Invisible Visits

Invisible Visits

Black Middle-Class Women in the American Healthcare System

TINA K. SACKS

Assistant Professor,
University of California, Berkeley

OXFORD
UNIVERSITY PRESS

OXFORD

UNIVERSITY PRESS

Oxford University Press is a department of the University of Oxford. It furthers the University's objective of excellence in research, scholarship, and education by publishing worldwide. Oxford is a registered trade mark of Oxford University Press in the UK and certain other countries.

Published in the United States of America by Oxford University Press 198 Madison Avenue, New York, NY 10016, United States of America.

Library of Congress Cataloging-in-Publication Data
Names: Sacks, Tina K., 1972– author.
Title: Invisible visits : black middle-class women in the American healthcare system / Tina K. Sacks.
Description: New York, NY : Oxford University Press, [2019] |
Includes bibliographical references and index.
Identifiers: LCCN 2018027572 (print) | LCCN 2018042544 (ebook) |
ISBN 9780190840211 (updf) | ISBN 9780190840228 (epub) |
ISBN 9780190840235 (Online Component) |
ISBN 9780190840204 (preprinted case cover : alk. paper)
Subjects: LCSH: African American women—Medical care. |
African American women—Health and hygiene.
Classification: LCC RA564.86 (ebook) | LCC RA564.86 .S23 2019 (print) |
DDC 362.1089/96073—dc23
LC record available at https://lccn.loc.gov/2018027572

To my dear ancestors Dora and Dave; JB and Lucille

To my loving parents Bette and Stanley

To my gentle brother Drake

To my beloved Carlos, Benicio Zelig, and Lolo

CONTENTS

PROLOGUE

The motivation for this book began more than 15 years ago while I was working at the Centers for Disease Control and Prevention (CDC) in Atlanta. In the late '90s, Atlanta was a sultry, lush metropolis full of promise. A booming economy, low housing prices, and year-round warm weather had enticed many people, including many African Americans, to relocate to what was deemed the "New South."

Although Black professionals were still in the minority at CDC, I found many of my colleagues were much like myself: educated Black women, fresh from acquiring their graduate degrees. Beyond our professional interest in public health and medicine, we bonded over discussions of dating, managing our burgeoning careers, and our shared experience of being professional Black women. We were excited by the possibilities the job afforded, but even in the so-called New South, a graduate degree and a fancy job did not protect us from our colleagues' surprise at how articulate, well-read, or well-traveled we were. Today, we call these comments "microaggressions," but back then we knew of no such word.

During my time in Atlanta, I was a speechwriter and special assistant to the Director of the CDC, a federal agency with an impressive $6 billion budget. I was also frequently overlooked, ignored, or treated as though I were invisible. I would walk into meetings with my boss who, even though there was only one other person present, wouldn't bother to introduce me. I became so used to receding into the background that one day when she sternly reprimanded me for accidently bumping into her suitcase, it barely registered when she said, "be careful with my bag, *Sherpa*."

Sherpa? A graduate degree from the University of Chicago had qualified me to write the very words this woman testified before the US Congress, but, in her mind, and in the minds of many others, I was nothing more than a servant, a lackey, a Sherpa. Of course, I could not be certain whether the fact that I am a mixed-race Black woman had anything to do with why she was so quick to diminish me. At the time, I was the only Black professional woman working in the Director's office in the upper echelons of the agency. In fact, I was pretty much always the only one no matter what office.

Although my Black female colleagues were scattered throughout the agency, we rarely encountered each other in a professional capacity. But we often got together to eat and drink; sharing the confusing experiences we had at work, at the store, or at the doctor. Confusing because we could never know whether we were treated differently because of racism, sexism, or the particular combination of both reserved exclusively for Black women.

During one of these dinners, the conversation turned to similar terrain, but, unlike other nights, that evening unearthed the observation that would ultimately lead to this book.

Our friend Angela had recently gone to a consultation with a new ob-gyn. She offhandedly mentioned that she was careful to make sure her CDC badge was visible over her clothes for as long as possible before she disrobed. Angela quipped that the badge communicated volumes without a single word. It let the doctor know she had an education and a good job that required specialized knowledge of medical terminology.

Lo and behold, that evening we realized we had all used the same strategy. We laughed at the absurdity of trying to keep our work badges on during a doctor's visit, but we knew we were using that badge strategically, to convey our intelligence. To show that we were Black but not poor. That we were women, but weren't hysterical. And finally, that we had "good" employer-sponsored health insurance. In other words, we were playing against type. But perhaps, most importantly, without speaking it aloud, implicitly we knew we had to work hard to get the best care possible.

Later, while I was getting my PhD, I learned more about racial and gender differences in treatment, but the studies focused almost exclusively on poor African Americans. And, yet, I met so many Black women who were not poor but had more than a sneaking suspicion that their experience at the doctor was quite different from that of White women.

As these ideas were beginning to take shape, I sought the expertise of a health disparities researcher who was a Black woman, physician, and professor of medicine at a prestigious university. We talked about my research ideas, which seemed to resonate with her recent experience giving birth to twins. She described being denied pain medications during labor even after repeatedly asking for them. The nurses and other physicians refused her until she told them she was an attending physician in a different ward of the same hospital. Disparities in pain management, as it turns out, are among the largest and most persistent racial disparities in the US healthcare system.

The more I read, I found study after study documenting how racial discrimination negatively affected treatment; yet, there were few studies about the persistence of racial and gender discrimination for non-poor Blacks. It was as if middle-class status could buy you out of being an African American woman. Or at least render you invisible to researchers.

Contrary to the rhetoric of the so-called post-racial era, the women in this book highlight the persistence of many forms of discrimination regardless of class status. Focusing on women of color who are not poor and who continue to face bias and discrimination when dealing with doctors suggests that our nation's healthcare system has a long way to go. The differential and spotty treatment of Black middle-class women certainly does not bode well for how vulnerable people—low-income, non–English speakers, immigrants—fare in the US healthcare system. What's more, their treatment begs the notion that the problem we have with health disparities may well go far beyond what our current research tells us. Ultimately, Black middle-class women may indeed be a litmus test for how well our healthcare system functions for everyone.

Introduction

On several occasions I have felt as if my doctor is dismissive or makes assumptions about me because I'm a single Black woman. Ob-gyns weren't interested in hearing my concerns about the pill or willing to answer questions about an IUD. Right now, I can't remember all the circumstances when I felt like a poor pregnant teenager in Washington. All I remember was how often I left the office feeling angry and confused. I would go into doctor's appointments with my guard up, ready to give a run down of my pedigree so that they would know that they were dealing with someone who was informed, not ignorant. And the crazy thing is, that I definitely remember this happening with both Black female docs and White men. So you just don't know who you'll connect with or what kind of stereotypes they have of you when you walk through the door. Eventually, I just stopped going to the doctor because I got so tired of feeling frustrated when I walked out.

—Cherie, a Washington, DC-based journalist, recounts her experiences with healthcare providers

— must play up class in order to survive

Invisible Visits tells the story of middle-class Black women whose experiences of race and gender discrimination in healthcare settings are all but overlooked in social science research. Through interviews and focus groups with these women, I analyze how the perception of bias and stereotyping affect healthcare for Black women who are not poor but who remain socially and economically vulnerable nonetheless. I argue that these women anticipate being stereotyped and often feel they have to emphasize hard-won skills, like their education or careers, to push back against their physicians' biased or discriminatory views.

not just y'all. is valid

If Cherie's experience is any indication, going to the doctor often requires forethought, strategy, and great effort. Cherie and I were childhood friends who went to a private prep school on Chicago's South Side. Although we were two Black girls in a private high school, Cherie and I nevertheless had very different upbringings. Cherie's father had been the first Black person to attend a prominent southern law school and later went on to hold leadership positions in the city government of Gary, Indiana. In the late 1980s, reeling from the waning steel industry, Gary's middle-class population, both Black and White, was rapidly declining. But Cherie's family was safely ensconced in one of the remaining Black middle-class enclaves.

— harder if have PPD!

I remember one of the first times I made the 40-minute drive from Chicago to Gary to visit her. The neighborhood seemed similar to my own, with its neat lawns and single-family homes. The interior of the house was like a perfectly coifed woman. There was not a throw pillow or framed photo out of place. The powder room was adorned with monogrammed guest towels and delicate, untouched soap in a beautiful dish. Although I was also ostensibly middle class, I did not grow up with such orderly attention to detail. The soap in my house was encrusted with dried bubbles, evidence of the previous hands that had used it. By contrast, Cherie's house was a symbol of the people who lived in it: fancy, fashionable, and established.

Ironically, even to me, Cherie was somewhat of a unicorn. She was both undeniably culturally Black and upper middle class. Although I was also Black and middle class, my family and my life were markedly different. Cherie's family was the kind that took excursions to the Caribbean with other similarly situated family friends and made weekend trips to football games at historically Black colleges. She was somehow both Black and able to take ski trips to Colorado with the White kids with whom we went to school. She didn't even need to code switch,[1] she simply moved seamlessly between the worlds she inhabited. Perhaps this had something to do with her mother, who was young and glamorous and deeply connected to all the right people. In fact, Cherie debuted at a cotillion sponsored by a local chapter of Jack and Jill, a national organization started in 1938 to help middle- and upper-class Black children remain connected to Black culture and identity.

The notion that there were enough upper middle-class Black people to form 230 US chapters of their own club was not something that occurred to me before I met Cherie. I grew up middle class in an interracial, interfaith family with a Black mother and a White, Jewish father. As an interracial family in the 1970s and '80s, we were still something of a taboo and certainly outside the norm. My mother, a Black woman who grew up very poor in the Jim Crow South, knew nothing of the insular upper-crusty Black community that gathered in Jack and Jill meetings. My father grew up with parents who emigrated from Eastern Europe and spoke Yiddish as their primary language. Like children of many immigrant families, my father did well in school and became a lawyer, although my grandparents never learned to read or write in English. Given this backdrop, it's probably not surprising that no one in my family could have envisioned that there were many young women like Cherie in major cities around the country.

---

[1] Code-switching is the practice of alternating between two languages or styles of language in conversation. The term often connotes the process through which ethno- racial minorities use different language or colloquialisms depending on the racial or cultural background of the person with whom they are speaking or the context (Anderson, 2000).

And, yet, Cherie and I ended up in the same high school and were close friends for years. She went on to attend a tony private university on the East Coast and ultimately earned a master's degree at the London School of Economics. We would both likely be characterized as middle class in spite of what seemed like substantial differences in our upbringing and adult socioeconomic status (SES). But, if we were to rely on popular renderings of Black women, one would think that people like Cherie and I didn't exist. Or that, if we did, our experiences in the world would be exactly the same. In many ways, Cherie's experience planted the seed for this book long before I even knew anything about healthcare disparities. This book uses qualitative methods in original research with Black middle-class women like Cherie to understand their experiences overall and to illuminate their experiences at the doctor's office, in particular.

For example, in spite of Cherie's pedigree, her comments suggest she often had to deal with doctors' unnamed set of stereotypes about Black women: angry, loud, promiscuous like the "sista" girl from around the way or the fraudulent users of government benefits (i.e., "welfare queens"). The list of negative characterizations of Black women is easy to find in American culture and society. In fact, the former First Lady Michelle Obama's depiction in the media represents one of the most striking examples of stereotyping of Black women regardless of class status. Mrs. Obama was often characterized as an "angry Black woman," a trope that followed her to the White House in spite of her Ivy League education, career, and social position.[2] If former First Lady Michelle Obama's experience is any guide, Black women of any class remain vulnerable to the specific racist and sexist antipathy/stereotypes some scholars call *misogynoir*.[3]

I argue that these stereotypes follow them into the doctor's office as well. What Cherie and others like her experience at the doctor's office is an extension of the general sense of illegitimacy that taints Black Americans regardless of class status. One of the more durable stereotypes is the notion that most Black people live in ghettos or are poor and uneducated. This is a prevailing and purposeful myth designed to erase the contours, context, and humanity of Black Americans as a whole. Against this backdrop, Cherie's experience suggests that she and the other Black middle-class women I interviewed feel the need to go to the doctor with their guard up. From the moment they approach the receptionist to the

---

[2] See *New Yorker* cover https://www.theguardian.com/world/2008/jul/15/barackobama.usa) http://www.thedailybeast.com/articles/2012/01/13/michelle-obama-confronts-racial-stereotypes-in-white-house-tell-all.html).

[3] "Misogynoir" is a term first coined by Professor Moya Bailey to describe the specific way racism and sexism combine to oppress Black women: "Misogynoir describes the co- constitutive, anti-Black, and misogynistic racism directed at Black women, particularly in visual and digital culture" (Bailey, 2016, p. 1).

weigh-in with the triage nurse, women feel they must emphasize their education, upbringing, or career, in an effort to counterbalance the pervasive, demeaning, stereotyping they face.

Cherie, for example, catalogued the adjustments she made during visits with the doctor. They ranged from highlighting her education to her efforts to make her own reproductive healthcare decisions. Yet all of these adjustments were not enough to overcome the deeply ingrained stereotypes held by male, female, Black, and White healthcare providers. She also noted that doctors viewed her in the same highly stigmatized way that they viewed a "poor, pregnant teenager." Of course, having children early and outside of marriage is another persistent stereotype of Black women, one that plays on underlying assumptions of Black lasciviousness and irresponsibility (Benkert & Peters, 2005). As a result of her frustration, Cherie eventually stopped going to the doctor all together.

Curtailing medical care, in and of itself, should be cause for concern. And may in part explain why Black women have worse health outcomes than their White counterparts (Jackson & Cummings, 2011; Jacobs, Rolle, Ferrans, Whitaker, & Warnecke, 2006; LaVeist, Nuru-Jeter, & Jones, 2003). It is also unclear how women make decisions about avoiding the doctor. Would they eschew going to the doctor even if they had a serious or life-threatening condition? In Cherie's case, she needed a specific form of contraception that seemed unpopular with physicians during that time period.[4] Cherie's experience suggests that we just do not know how women make decisions about not seeing their doctor or when it may negatively affect their health. But it implicates bias and stereotyping as a main driver of healthcare disparities, especially among Black middle-class women who are not poor and who have health insurance (Earnshaw et al., 2016; Harris et al., 2006; Pascoe & Smart Richman, 2009).

Furthermore, Cherie's statement highlights another way stereotyping may affect Black people's health. She notes that even in her encounters with Black female physicians she felt as though she was being stereotyped as a poor pregnant teenager. Although the research about interventions to end differences in treatment emphasizes having Black patients seek treatment from Black doctors, Cherie's experience hints at the inherent problem with using that strategy alone. One of the most pernicious effects of stereotypes is that they also affect the self-concept of the target group. For example, some women have stereotypical views of women's intellectual capacities (Steele, 1997), and some Black people have internalized the stereotype that other Black people are lazy or don't want to work (Frost, 2011). In fact, Claude Steele, the psychologist who developed the

[4] More recently, reproductive justice scholars have argued that healthcare providers disproportionately prescribe long-acting reversible contraception (LARCs) like IUDs or Norplant to Black and Latina women (Downey, Arteaga, Villaseñor, & Gomez, 2017).

concept of stereotype threat, found that Black people, women, and other groups who are often the targets of negative stereotyping eventually internalize them. His studies noted that when women were primed with a stereotypical depiction of women's poor math ability, they actually performed worse on math tests (Steele, 1997). The same was true of Black people (Steele & Aronson, 1995). Steele's research indicates that the targets of the stereotype may come to view themselves through that same lens.

In a similar vein, many scholars have written about internalized racism in which minorities come to view themselves from the perspective of the dominant society (Fanon, 1952). The legendary sociologist, W. E. B. DuBois (1903) characterized the experience of Black people in America as one of "double consciousness," in which Black people come to view themselves from the perspective of the White society that dominated them. DuBois (1903) notes, "It is a peculiar sensation, this double-consciousness, this sense of always looking at one's self through the eyes of others, of measuring one's soul by the tape of a world that looks on in amused contempt and pity" (p. 3).

Finally, as I argue throughout the book, stereotypes and bias must be understood in the broader context of structural discrimination. In other words, in trying to understand healthcare disparities, it is important to go beyond the individual-level interaction between provider and patient. As psychiatrist Jonathan M. Metzl (2010) argues in his book *The Protest Psychosis: How Schizophrenia Became a Black Disease*, "racial tensions are structured into clinical interactions long before doctors or patients enter examining rooms" (p. xi). He also notes that our interventions to reduce disparities fail when they "focus exclusively on the race of the patient and of the doctor, and define the problem as arising in the intersection of these two races" (Metzl, 2010, p. xiii).

Metzl's framing of the clinical interaction illuminates Cherie's experience with both Black and White physicians. Given that Black and female providers certainly may hold stereotypical views of their patients, interventions to end healthcare disparities must address the broader context. Furthermore, while increasing the proportion of Black and female healthcare providers is much needed, addressing Black and female experiences of discrimination in healthcare should not stop there.[5] Rather, we need to go further in attending to the multiple structural causes of differences in treatment.

[5] Striving to ensure patients and providers are matched on race, ethnicity, gender, and/or language preference, also termed "race and gender concordance" in the research literature (LaVeist, Nuru-Jeter, & Jones, 2003), has long been one of the preferred strategies to reduce differences in treatment.

All told, Cherie's story points to enduring fissures in the US healthcare system, which motivate the questions that guide this book:

- How does race and gender, particularly race and gender stereotypes, bias, and discrimination, affect Black middle-class women's healthcare treatment?
- Why do Black middle-class women continue to receive less than standard treatment and often have poorer health outcomes than their white counterparts?
- How do historical experiences of racial and gender discrimination affect Black women's contemporary engagement with healthcare providers?

The Problem: Health and Healthcare Disparities Among the Black Middle Class

Health Outcome Disparities

Despite Black Americans economic mobility gains, members of the Black middle class are still disproportionately more sick and die earlier than their White counterparts. In fact, Black–White disparities in health outcomes in the United States have been present and extensively studied for years (Krieger, 2001a; 2002; 2005; Krieger & Sidney, 1996; LaVeist et al., 2003). Black Americans are at higher risk for many chronic, debilitating conditions including diabetes, hypertension, cardiovascular disease, and certain cancers (Abell et al., 2008; Hershman et al., 2005; Jackson et al., 2014; Reeder-Hayes & Anderson, 2017; Saydah, Imperatore, Cheng, Geiss, & Albright, 2017). However, many public health studies documenting these inequities fail to account for the many structural factors that affect individual health and instead rely on biological determinants, which may further the myth of racial essentialism (Hatch, 2016). Health indices such as overall mortality rates and infant mortality rates point to systematic inequalities in health between Blacks and Whites (Braveman & Barclay, 2009; Geronimus, 1996).

One of the most important systematic inequalities is unequal access to material resources like income and wealth, which may lead to poor health behaviors, chronic health conditions, and diseases (Phelan, Link, & Tehranifar, 2010). Scholars have known for decades that health and well-being are closely related to SES (Deaton, 2002; Marmot, Kogevinas, & Elston, 1987; Waitzkin, 2000). However, in studies that adjust statistically for socioeconomic resources, Black–White health disparities do not disappear (Pollack et al., 2007; Williams, 1999). This represents somewhat of a paradox that Black people, regardless of their material resources, cannot "buy" the same health as their White counterparts. For many Black middle-class folk, simply being as healthy as the majority middle class remains stubbornly out of reach.

We also know that Blacks of middle-class status share a disproportionate burden of illness and premature death, also termed "morbidity and mortality," compared to Whites. For instance, college-educated Black women still have infant mortality rates that are twice that of their college-educated White counterparts (Mullings & Wali, 2001). To really appreciate the magnitude of that fact, we must consider several contextual factors.

First, the United States is the most advanced industrialized economy in the world, yet the nation's infant mortality rate remains higher than most other developed countries (Mathews, MacDorman, & Thoma, 2015). In fact, the United States ranks 26th out of 29 member countries of the Organization for Economic Cooperation and Development (OECD), behind most European countries and Japan, Korea, Israel, New Zealand, and Australia (Osterman & Martin, 2014). Black infant mortality is a big reason the United States lags behind its economic counterparts in this important health indicator (Giscombé & Lobel, 2005). Although Black infant mortality recently declined (Osterman & Martin, 2014), Black babies are still more than twice as likely to die before their first birthday than White babies.

Importantly, Black women with a college degree are more likely to lose an infant before it reaches its first year than White women with much less education. In a society in which health status is so closely related to educational attainment (Braveman, Cubbin, Marchi, Egerter, & Chavez, 2001), the fact that Black women with much more education fare worse than White women with less is striking. The question, of course, is why. Some scholars suggest that underlying genetic differences between Blacks and Whites explains the disparity, while many critical scholars reject biologically determined explanations outright (Bediako, BeLue, & Hillemeier, 2015; David & Collins, 2007; Duster, 2005; Hatch, 2016; Obasogie, Harris-Wai, Darling, Keagy, & Levesque, 2014). Still other scholars note that the social environment, and particularly the race and gender discrimination Black women face, is the most likely cause (Anachebe, 2006; Wallace, Green, Richardson, Theall, & Crear-Perry, 2017). To date, the research points to chronic stress as a result of long-term exposure to race and gender discrimination (Kramer, Hogue, Dunlop, & Menon, 2011). In other words, Black women are affected by systemic discrimination regardless of their class status, which may ultimately harm their developing fetus.

Another striking difference between Blacks and Whites are wealth disparities. At every level of income, the differences in wealth between African Americans and Whites are large, pervasive, and widely documented (Oliver & Shapiro, 2006; Shapiro, 2004). For example, the median wealth (assets minus debts) of White households is 20 times that of Black households (Kochhar, Fry, Taylor, Velasco, & Motel, 2011). In 2009, the median wealth of Black families was $5,677 while White families had a median wealth of $113,149

(Kochhar, Fry, Taylor, Velasco, & Motel, 2011). This is more than a matter of not being able to save money to pass on to future generations, although that is certainly problematic. The economic foundation of middle-class Blacks is substantially more precarious than Whites. On average, Black people do not have the savings to weather economic downturns, to take vacations to reduce their stress, or to carry them through an unexpected job loss.

Given this backdrop, Black Americans often expend significant effort to acquire additional financial security. This ultimately may lead African Americans to pay the mental health costs of upward social mobility (Cole & Omari, 2003). Furthermore, stressors such as racial discrimination may diminish their returns on their education, training, and other human capital investments, which limits their financial capabilities (Hudson et al., 2012).

Here, again, we see middle-class Black Americans face additional challenges and stressors as they try to solidify the economic foundation of their families.

Unequal Treatment: How Provider Biases Contribute to Healthcare Disparities

In addition to differences in health outcomes (i.e., differences in life expectancy, infant mortality, etc.), inequities persist even after people arrive at the doctor's office. In the early 2000s, against a backdrop of growing concern about healthcare disparities, the Institute of Medicine (IOM) conducted a groundbreaking study to understand the causes and consequences of the problem (Nelson, Stith, & Smedley, 2002). The study documented widespread and pervasive differences in the way ethno-racial minorities were treated in medical settings.

They found that people of color did not receive the standard of care for many health conditions regardless of their health insurance status or ability to pay for treatment (Nelson et al., 2002). The study became one of the seminal works in the field of healthcare disparities and launched a cascade of follow-up studies to better understand how the interaction between the patient and provider contributes to differences in treatment. The IOM study, and the voluminous body of evidence that emerged in its wake, suggested that physician bias, whether conscious or unconscious, is a main driver of differences in treatment (Hall et al., 2015; Nelson et al., 2002). Ethnic and racial minorities, women, and others from vulnerable social positions are particularly vulnerable to bias and stereotyping (Williams, 2012). Numerous studies have documented that healthcare providers are unconsciously or unintentionally biased against members of marginalized groups, which ultimately leads to differences in treatment across multiple domains (i.e., specialty care, pain management, mental health services, etc.; Aronson, Burgess, Phelan, & Juarez, 2013; Burgess, Fu, & Van

Ryn, 2004; Van Ryn & Fu, 2003). Even though physicians often report an aversion to racial or gender biases, empirical tests of physician attitudes and behavior find that healthcare providers certainly have negative feelings or evaluations of their patients based on their race, gender, and other factors (FitzGerald & Hurst, 2017). Analyses of unconscious (implicit) biases find that these forms of bias are relatively common (FitzGerald & Hurst, 2017; Penner et al., 2010).

For example, a large body of evidence indicates that Black people are systematically undertreated for pain compared to Whites (Hoffman, Trawalter, Axt, & Oliver, 2016). Healthcare providers often underestimate and undertreat Black people's pain (Hoffman et al., 2016). These differences even extend to Black children who present in emergency departments for acute appendicitis (Goyal, Kuppermann, Cleary, Teach, & Chamberlain, 2015). In a study that reviewed almost 1 million cases of appendicitis in the United States, Black children were less likely to receive any type of pain management for moderate pain and less likely to receive opiates for severe pain (Goyal et al., 2015).

Incredibly, a 2015 study of more than 400 medical students and residents found that differences in pain management may be explained by the fact that providers believe Blacks are fundamentally biologically different from Whites.[6] The study found half of medical students and residents endorsed the erroneous idea that Blacks' nerve endings are less sensitive than Whites and that Whites have larger brains than Blacks. Importantly, this study also found that students and residents who endorsed false beliefs also inaccurately evaluated the pain of Black patients in simulations of pain evaluation and treatment. The misevaluation of pain ultimately led to less accurate treatment recommendations for the Black patients as compared to Whites (Goyal et al., 2015).

Given that we know physicians' negative evaluations of members of a group may lead to healthcare disparities regardless of the patient's class status, scholars are beginning to focus on differences in treatment that affect the Black middle class. For example, one of the world's most prominent health disparities researchers, sociologist David Williams, and his colleagues strongly emphasize that race matters even after class status is taken into account (Williams, Priest, & Anderson, 2016). Williams has also called for more attention to how the factors that can negatively or positively affect or improve health are systematically

---

[6] Much of biomedical science, research, and training implicitly rests on the notion of racial dimorphism, or the fundamental biological differences between Blacks, Whites, and other groups (Hatch, 2016; Krieger, 1987; Obasogie et al., 2014). In fact, I would argue, that much of the health disparities literature approaches differences in health outcomes from this biologically determined, essentialist point of view, even when many of these same researchers purport to subscribe to a social constructionist explanation of race (Ford, 2016). The implications of this perspective will be explored further in Chapter 4.

patterned by race, ethnicity, and SES. This means that exposure to the toxic stress of financial insecurity or inadequate access to healthy food is not equally distributed in American society. It depends on one's race, gender, and class status. The same is true of resources that promote health, like clean air and adequate household income (Jackson & Williams, 2006).

For example, we know that Black people may still be treated differently at the doctor and have worse mental health outcomes than their White counterparts regardless of their class status (Hudson, Neighbors, Geronimus, & Jackson, 2016; Jackson & Cummings, 2011; Williams, Mohammed, Leavell, & Collins, 2010). In addition to physical health outcomes, Hudson and colleagues have found that middle-class Blacks are at even greater risk than their poorer counterparts for mental health problems associated with exposure to racial discrimination (Hudson et al., 2016). Although Americans typically think of acquiring education as the way to a better life, researchers have found that greater levels of education were associated with increased levels of racial discrimination and depression (Hudson et al., 2016). This research supports Williams et al.'s (Williams, 1999; Williams & Collins, 1995) work documenting the fact that, although Black middle-class health improves with additional SES resources, Black people do not receive the same health protections as their White counterparts. This has also been called the "diminishing returns" hypothesis, in which Farmer and Ferraro (2005) found that Black people actually receive declining health returns as SES (i.e., education) increases. In other words, it seems that, for Black Americans, acquiring more education leads to more opportunities to be discriminated against, which ultimately is bad for one's health.

Perhaps due to his own experience in acquiring education, sociologist and health disparities researcher Sherman James recognized the potentially deleterious effect of striving for upward mobility while Black. James observed that Black people who worked tirelessly to gain economic or education resources actually had worse health outcomes, particularly with regard to hypertension, than their White counterparts (James, Strogatz, Wing, & Ramsey, 1987). James called this relentless striving in the face of structural barriers "John Henryism," harkening back to American folklore in which a Southern Black man of remarkable strength and endurance suddenly collapsed and died after years of overwork. James, himself a Black man who endured overt racial discrimination in the American South, noted that John Henryism was caused by the indecency of daily racial discrimination and Black people's effort to cope with it (James, 1994).

Stereotyping and the Healthcare Encounter

In addition to high-effort coping and exposure to racial discrimination, the pernicious effects of stereotyping may help to explain mental and physical health disparities that persist for the Black middle class. Scholars have long noted that stereotyping is a critical component of a system that creates racist subordination (Omi & Winant, 1994). Stereotyping may also negatively affect health through both interpersonal pathways, such as increasing hypervigilance and allostatic load, and structural pathways, such as perpetuating unhealthy social and physical environments (e.g., public transportation systems) that degrade and devalue Black health (Kwate & Meyer, 2011). Black women experience the healthcare system in the context of pervasive negative stereotypes about their race and gender, including the angry Black woman, mammy, welfare queen, and prostitute (Harris-Perry, 2011). In describing the particular stereotypes Black women face in the United States, noted Black feminist scholar Patricia Hill Collins (2000) also theorizes the connection between stereotyping and oppression:

> From the mammies, jezebels, and breeder women of slavery to the smiling Aunt Jemimas on pancake mix boxes, ubiquitous Black prostitutes, and ever-present welfare mothers of contemporary popular culture, negative stereotypes applied to African-American women have been fundamental to Black women's oppression. (p. 7)

In addition to Collins, psychologists Charise Jones and Kumea Shorter-Gooden analyzed the specific challenges Black women face in their seminal book on how Black women experience American society. Jones and Shorter-Gooden found that Black women are routinely confined to caricatures that are grotesque, narrow, and unfair (Jones & Shorter-Gooden, 2003). Furthermore, intersectional scholars who study how race and gender join to create unique conditions informed by multiple, overlapping identities have long noted that Black women face the double bind of Blackness and womanhood (Collins, 2000; Crenshaw, 1991; Samuels & Ross-Sheriff, 2008). Their experiences cannot be understood through either the lens of race or gender in isolation, but at the intersection of these identities.

In spite of the pervasiveness of negative stereotypes of Black women, relatively few works of social science consider how stereotyping contributes to a far less than ideal healthcare environment. The work of medical sociologist Janet Shim, who conceptualizes the healthcare encounter as a transaction between patient and provider, may help us understand how Black women approach the particular challenges of the healthcare encounter (Shim, 2010).

Rooted in noted sociologist Pierre Bourdieu's concept of *habitus*, cultural health capital theorizes that one's ability to reproduce certain cultural actions is central to the patient–provider interaction (Shim, 2010). Shim defines this form of capital as a specialized collection of cultural skills, attitudes, behaviors, and interactional styles that are valued, leveraged, and exchanged by both patients and providers during clinical interactions. These skills and resources may include styles of dress, verbal skills, scientific knowledge, educational credentials, and healthcare literacy. Cultural health capital is also rooted in the historical and cultural moment, which emphasizes patient consumerism, initiative, and self-surveillance.

For Black middle-class women, elements of cultural health capital are particularly relevant. For example, Shim notes that cultural health capital rests on one's ability to communicate social privilege and resources that can act as cues of favorable social and economic status and consumer savvy. To establish these resources, patients must demonstrate knowledge of medical topics and vocabulary and also have the ability to convey healthcare information to the provider in an efficient and rational manner. All of these skills are critical to a successful healthcare encounter. Cultural health capital presupposes a belief in the value of, and resources to, practice self-discipline and the ability to take an instrumental attitude toward the body. Given that Black people are often reduced to caricatures about laziness, lack of intelligence, and the like, demonstrating one's cultural health capital may be characterized of as a form of resistance to stereotyping (Sacks, 2017).

Importantly, although cultural health capital suggests that patients may indeed possess the resources to manage the healthcare encounter, these transactions may come at a cost. Shim posits that cultural health capital may contribute to the accumulation of power and the persistence of inequality (Shim, 2010). For example, in a study of how healthcare providers think about their patients, researchers found that they have particular expectations of what makes a capable and proficient patient (Dubbin, Chang, & Shim, 2013). Patients who do not meet the provider's expectation of astute self-management are considered less appealing all together, causing a rupture in the patient–provider relationship (Dubbin et al., 2013).

Although the dominant paradigm in American medicine emphasizes the importance of physician objectivity and scientific rationality, this research highlights the obvious: physicians are human beings replete with foibles and subject to the same socialization that reinforces stereotypes as anyone else. We know that physicians are not immune to bias and stereotyping, but few scholarly works have explored how Black women perceive and respond to it or how it affects the healthcare encounter overall. Given the pervasive stereotypes of Black women, they may feel even more pressure to emphasize certain elements of such capital in the hopes of connecting with their physicians and mitigating prevailing notions of Black female illegitimacy (Sacks, 2017).

The analysis of Black women's experience in healthcare settings rests on an understanding of the impact of stereotyping, including the concept of stereotype threat, as well as with the socially distributed set of resources Black women may use to mitigate these threats. This book delineates the conditions under which women feel they need to counter such stereotypes, the burden they experience in enacting these behaviors, and the potentially negative effects on their health. Finally, the work provides an in-depth exploration of *how* Black women actually perceive the healthcare encounter and healthcare providers and considers the situational adjustments women make to advocate on their own behalf. In so doing, the book is among the first to analyze how implicit and explicit bias affects women and leads to differences in treatment and health disparities. Moreover, the book avoids the dominant paradigm in public health research, one that uses a neo-liberal frame to blame individuals for their worse health outcomes (Chowkwanyun, 2011; Krieger, 2001a). By placing the contemporary experience of the Black middle class in a historical context, this book also describes how pervasive stereotyping coupled with scientific racism has led to poor treatment in (and as a result of) cases such as the Tuskegee Syphilis Experiment and the Mississippi Appendectomy (a term used to denote the eugenic practice of overuse of hysterectomy among African American women). These forms of medical maltreatment are often reinstantiated in contemporary forms of discrimination in healthcare settings, as reflected in disparities in hysterectomy rates, pain management, and mental health treatment.

Method

To analyze this topic, I conducted interviews and focus groups in 2010 and 2011 with a total of 30 African American middle-class women in Chicago. At the onset, I set out to better understand subtle intraracial class differences in the healthcare experiences of lower middle-class Black women relative to upper middle-class Black women.[7] Given that the research literature focuses almost exclusively on the Black poor and, to a lesser extent, on the lower middle class[i], I wanted to explore how differences in class/SES affect Black women's engagement with healthcare providers. I knew that because SES categories are notoriously messy

---

[7] Although the study was initially designed to better understand intraracial class variation in the healthcare experiences of Black women, the findings suggested that lower middle- and upper middle-class Black women had very similar healthcare experiences related to pervasive stereotyping based on race and gender. As such, this book focuses on Black middle-class women as a whole.

and hard to define (Braveman et al., 2001; Conley, 2010), a Black woman who is an administrative assistant with an associate's degree and a Black woman with an MBA making six figures would likely both be considered "middle class" based on their income, education, and occupation (Pattillo, 2013). However, it is unclear whether the relative difference in socioeconomic position leads to different experiences in the world and in healthcare settings. As such, this research was designed to break out an underresearched subset of Black women and, in turn, understand how they experience healthcare settings from these markedly different positions.

Taking the argument a step further, an explicit purpose of this book is to explore intragroup variation among African Americans. Although healthcare disparities studies are explicitly concerned with Black–White comparisons, this work focuses solely on African Americans. Moreover, it contributes to research that makes sense of similarities and differences between Black people who may share a similar racial phenotype or purported Black identity but are likely to differ ideologically, politically, socially, and economically. This body of research, including scholarship by Cathy Cohen, Melissa Harris-Perry, Mary Patillo, Karyn Lacy, and others, analyzes within-group variation in Black political thought, social behavior, and life outcomes. The work of these scholars provides the precedent for the in-depth study of African Americans as a group unto themselves.

A secondary purpose of this work, in which I move away from studying African Americans in comparison to Whites, is to carve out more space to explore how race, class, and gender affect Black women in healthcare settings. Limiting the study to African Americans facilitates understanding (1) the lived experience of class and racial status among non-poor Black people, (2) variation within the Black middle class, and (3) how Black people relate to each other on matters of class, racial identity, and racial authenticity. Moreover, understanding the factors that affect healthcare interactions among the Black middle class contributes to our overall understanding of healthcare disparities, as well as suggesting new possibilities for intervention.

Based on findings from these data, I make the following core claims, which will be explicated in the remainder of the book. First, stereotyping and race and gender discrimination persists across SES. Contrary to the dominant post-racial paradigm, race and gender discrimination continues to affect people even when they are not poor. Second, trying to resist stereotyping, bias, and discrimination can be exhausting, stressful, and may contribute to health problems (in a similar vein to the high-effort coping termed "John Henryism"; James, 1994). Third, although enacting specific strategies, including emphasizing one's career, intelligence, or health literacy, is sometimes stressful, women purposely use these tactics as forms of resistance despite their oft deleterious effects. As evidenced by the empirical data presented in the book, trying to advocate for oneself necessitates walking a fine line. Black women may emphasize their social status to disrupt implicit and explicit provider stereotyping, yet displaying too much knowledge and self-advocacy may backfire if providers think their patients are too pushy or noncompliant.

Given the power difference between patients and providers, this form of resistance does not always produce its intended effect and may ultimately hinder the patient's ability to attend to important information. Moreover, the intent of this work is not to suggest that women should bear the responsibility of strategizing to receive high-quality, unbiased, equitable healthcare. On the contrary: the work reorients us to the structural constraints that give rise to healthcare disparities in the first place. Fourth, minorities who are not poor, particularly Black middle-class women, are often overlooked in research. Yet by studying this group, we can isolate and better understand the persistence of race and gender discrimination and its relationship to class status. Fifth, historical instances of medical maltreatment and discrimination cast a long shadow on the contemporary healthcare experience of Black middle-class women and should be more thoroughly integrated into social science research on disparities. Finally, I argue that, given the overwhelming persistence of disparities, it is long past time to do something about them. Taken together, the evidence suggests that the healthcare experiences of Black women do not vary across SES in the same way that we see for White women. That is, the experience of White middle-class and poor women is likely very different, but Black women's experience does not seem to vary by class status to the same degree.

Rather than questioning why Black women's health outcomes are not the same as other populations, this book renders visible the intricacies and intimacies of the lives of Black women as they interact with the American healthcare system.

Plan of the Book

What follows is an investigation of the ways in which Black women who are not poor adapt, resist, and are shaped by race and gender discrimination, particularly in healthcare settings. Chapter 1 lays the groundwork for our understanding of the particular strengths and vulnerabilities of the Black middle class, especially Black middle-class women. In so doing, I describe why this group warrants consideration unto itself, review previous work on the Black middle class, and explore similarities and differences between the Black middle class, the Black poor, and the middle class in general. The chapter also provides an overview of stereotypes Black women face (e.g., the Mammy, Jezebel, and Sapphire), as well as *stereotype threat*, the situational predicament in which people are or feel themselves to be at risk of confirming negative stereotypes about their social group (Steele & Aronson, 1995). Finally, the chapter describes how Black women employ cultural health capital and other skills, such conducting research to prepare for a provider encounter, to resist negative stereotyping.

Chapter 2 outlines women's efforts to make connections with providers and ultimately secure quality treatment. I review how women use their cultural health capital, class resources, and self-presentation skills to advocate for themselves. The chapter also explores the impact of advocacy on the relationship between the provider and patient and develops the idea that self-advocacy may also be experienced as burdensome by the patient or pushy by the provider. This is particularly salient in an era of "patient-centered" medicine in which people are expected to advocate for themselves, thereby shifting the burden from the provider back to the patient.

Chapter 3 explores race and gender concordance as a strategy to mitigate stereotype threat and differences in treatment. I first introduce a case study, which describes the experiences of Tammy, a 42-year-old woman whose great-grandfather was killed as a result of his involuntary participation in the Tuskegee Syphilis Study. This case illustrates how past incidents of discrimination and trauma affect Black women's contemporary experience dealing with doctors. Then, the chapter reports on women's evaluation of the healthcare system overall as a rushed, impersonal, profit-driven enterprise that emphasizes money over clinical expertise, patient outcomes, and patient–provider trust. Finally, I analyze how Black women evaluate whether seeking a Black female provider leads to better care.

Chapter 4 examines contemporary reproductive healthcare in the context of pervasive stereotypes of Black women's purported physical hardiness. The chapter also provides a brief history of the overuse of hysterectomy, particularly in the American South, and details women's contemporary experience with hysterectomy as a treatment for uterine fibroids, a medical condition that disproportionately affects Black women of reproductive age.

The book concludes with Chapter 5, in which I argue that (1) racial and gender stereotypes negatively affect the healthcare experiences of Black middle-class women, (2) stereotyping is threatening regardless of whether healthcare providers hold conscious or unconscious biases about their patients, and (3) the threat of stereotyping certainly contributes to the US healthcare system's persistent problem with inequities in treatment. *Invisible Visits* concludes with recommendations for how healthcare providers and the healthcare system can explicitly acknowledge and mitigate these challenges by reorienting their focus to the structural causes of healthcare inequities (Metzl & Hansen, 2014).

1

The Black Middle Class
in White Space

Stereotyping and the Healthcare Encounter

One ever feels his two-ness,—an American, a Negro . . . two thoughts,
two unreconciled strivings; two warring ideals in one dark body, whose
dogged strength alone keeps it from being torn asunder.
—W. E. B. DuBois (1903)

Racism, specifically, is the state-sanctioned or extralegal production and
exploitation of group-differentiated vulnerability to premature death.
—Ruth Wilson Gilmore (2007)

Even before W. E. B. DuBois coined the term "double consciousness," Black
people in America have struggled to align their inner and outer lives (DuBois,
1903). Although this study was primarily concerned with an experience as mundane as a doctor's visit, respondents spoke of having to mask their internal feelings and present a calm and composed demeanor no matter how badly they felt
physically or psychically. The need to put one's best foot forward no matter the
circumstance is likely an adaption not just to the particulars of the American
healthcare environment, but also to the broader society that seems to lack empathy for the full range of the Black experience.

For example, a focus group respondent in her 50s recalled being socialized
from an early age to suppress her feelings, especially at the doctor:

> . . . . And look it, as African Americans, we were told—I was told—never
> to go to the doctor looking worn down and torn down, to always come
> together. But you think if I took the time to get myself together, I wasn't
> as sick? No. My mother told me to always have something together.

In this woman's experience, Black women are not allowed to be sick and tired
even though the doctor's office is ostensibly the place one should be able to let
one's guard down and fully explain one's condition to the provider. Her comments suggest that, for Black women, there is no room for vulnerability or even
an authentic expression of one's feelings. Yet the healthcare disparities literature

largely overlooks these contortions and the enormous toll they likely take on human health.

However, scholars in other disciplines, particularly sociologists Feagin and Sikes (1994) who examined daily racial indignities in *Living with Racism: The Black Middle Class Experience*, have explored how these contortions are related to the persistence of racism among middle-class Black people. Based on 209 in-depth interviews, Feagin and Sikes captured the machinations Black people enact to make it through the day. When asked what it was like to be a Black person in White America, one woman responded:

> One step from suicide! What I'm saying is—the psychological warfare games that we have to play everyday just to survive. We have to be one way in our communities and one way in the workplace or in the business sector. We can never be ourselves all around. I think that may be a given for all people but for us particularly; it's really a mental health problem. It's a wonder we haven't all gone out and killed somebody or killed ourselves. (Feagin & Sikes, 1994, p. vii)

While this respondent characterizes the toll being Black likely takes on her mental and physical health, geographer Ruth Wilson Gilmore points the finger squarely at racism as the mechanism that leads to premature death. In keeping with critical scholars like Gilmore, Feagin, and Sikes, I argue that the perception that one must constantly maneuver is bad for human health, whether or not that maneuvering is, in fact, required to avoid discrimination or secure proper healthcare treatment. Furthermore, as Gilmore argues, there is no amount of individual-level behavior modification or positive self-presentation that can undo the underlying reality of structural discrimination (Gilmore, 2007).

However, in spite of the persistence of racial discrimination as a determinant of health, many public health and health services researchers seem to focus almost exclusively on ethno- racial minorities who are poor, thereby ignoring the durability of racism across class. This myopia obscures the ways in which racial discrimination affects human health on its own. I argue that focusing on the Black middle class helps us understand the simultaneous privilege and marginalization faced by non-poor Black people, as well as the race-class-health relationship in general. Furthermore, because the Black middle class faces significant social and economic precariousness, some scholars have suggested that there is no true "Black middle class" (Conley, 2010). For example, Mary Pattillo and others have argued that the life chances of the Black middle class are more similar to the Black poor than to the White middle class (Landry, 1987; Pattillo, 2013). In contrast, Lacy and Cohen have focused on power and privilege among a relatively small percentage of Black elites at the top of the income and wealth distribution (Lacy, 2007).

The women whose stories appear throughout this book represent this intraracial class variation from lower middle to upper middle class. In so doing, the work breaks open the Black middle class to better understand the ways in which some of their life experiences appear more similar to poor Black people than to the White middle class, while, in other contexts (e.g., employment) they are undoubtedly advantaged relative to other Black people. To that end, I first briefly describe the Black middle class and explore the differences between the Black upper class, or "Black elite," as scholars Karyn Lacy and Cathy Cohen have described them, and the Black lower middle class, the group Mary Pattillo analyzed in *Black Picket Fences: Privilege and Peril Among the Black Middle Class* (2013).

Defining the (Black) Middle Class

Although much of American political discourse privileges the plight of the "middle class" there is no official government definition of what that term really means (Cashell, 2008). The question remains: what makes a person middle class? Possessing a college degree, maintaining a particular household income, or owning a home? Lay people and social scientists alike struggle to define "middle class" (Lareau & Conley 2008). Pattillo (2005) has noted that the term is usually based on a wide range of factors including income, education, and normative judgments about mores, values, or culture; household income of two to four times the federal poverty line by family size; the upper ranges of income groupings; or being a white-collar worker. That said, the income, occupational, and educational range of the middle class is broad and loosely defined (Pattillo, 2005).

For the purpose of this book, "middle class" is best understood as a constellation of factors, including education, wealth, income, and occupation. For example, the Pew Research Center uses income to define "middle class" and notes that households with incomes two-thirds to double the US median income after adjusting for household size fall into that category. In 2014, middle income ranged between $42,000 and $126,000 per year for a family of three (Pew Research Center, 2015). According to the Pew, approximately 45% of Black American households fall in that category (Pew Research Center, 2015).

The broad range of what is considered "middle class," or at least middle income, suggests a wide range of lived experiences among people who would be ostensibly categorized as middle class but whose day-to-day lives may differ substantively. For example, the majority of the Black middle class is likely

lower middle class, with life experiences that may be more akin to the working class (Pattillo, 2013). It is not hard to imagine that the lives of women making solid six-figure salaries like Bobbi (a 46-year-old finance executive with an
MBA) would be significantly different from Christina (a 43-year-old who runs
a home daycare business). Taking a closer look at within-group class differences
(i.e., between Black women who are lower middle class and those who are upper
middle class) is a central preoccupation of this book.[1]

However, it is critical to note that markers of socioeconomic success are not
equivalent between Black and White Americans. That is to say, although having
a college degree or high household income is typically indicative of a place in
the middle class, for Black people these accomplishments often lead to fewer
economic and social benefits than among the White middle class (Massey &
Denton, 1993; Pattillo, 2013; Thomas, 2015; Williams & Collins, 1995). For
example, African Americans are more likely to live in racially segregated neighborhoods with fewer amenities and are less wealthy than Whites of the same
income group (Conley, 1999; Isaacs & Schroder, 2004).

Regardless of how middle-class status is defined, recent data suggest that economic well-being among non-poor Black people confers simultaneous vulnerability and relative privilege. For example, a 2015 report on the American middle
class found that while Black adults experienced the largest income gains between
1971 and 2015, household income for Black families, including those at the top
of the income distribution, still lags behind White families overall (Pew Research
Center, 2015). In 2015, median income for Blacks in the top fifth of all Black
income earners was roughly equal to what their White counterparts earned in
1979 (i.e., $136,597 and $136,461, respectively). Moreover, Black families have
a more tenuous hold on middle-class status than their White counterparts, and
Black children are particularly vulnerable to downward socioeconomic mobility (Pew Research Center, 2015). More than half of Black Americans who were
middle class as children fall out of the middle class as adults, with many having
lower incomes than their parents (Pattillo, 2013). This may be due to the fact
that wealth disparities between African Americans and Whites are large and pervasive (Oliver and Shapiro, 2006; Shapiro, 2004), thus rendering the economic
foundation of middle class Blacks substantially more fragile than Whites. For
example, in 2009, the median net worth of White households was $113, 149
compared to only $5,677 for Black households (Kochhar, Fry, Taylor, Velasco,
& Motel, 2011). These data support a widely noted argument among scholars of
the Black middle class who often describe the Black and White middle classes as
"separate and unequal" (Pattillo, 2013, p. 2).

---

[1] A more detailed discussion of the research methods appears in the Methods appendix.

Black People in White Space: Stereotyping and the Healthcare Encounter

In spite of the growth of the post-Civil Rights Black middle class, American society is persistently segregated by race, leading to what sociologist Elijah Anderson describes as distinctly Black and White social environments, or Black and "white space." According to Anderson, these spaces emerge from an age-old American practice: segregation of Black and White people into separate social and physical worlds. Anderson argues that Black professionals often find themselves in work, school, or social settings in which they are the only Black person, an environment that typifies the "white space." Furthermore, Anderson notes that educated and accomplished Blacks are thought to be the exception to the rule, and their presence in predominately White spaces, like corporations or suburbs, is almost always considered provisional or requiring additional justification.

Anderson notes that institutional racism is often mediated through pervasive stereotyping of Black people in America. In other words, even in situations in which Black professionals have achieved a modicum of credibility, discrimination and stereotyping persist. Furthermore, although Anderson does not specifically address stereotypes levied at Black women, understanding the intersectional implications of how racism and sexism affect Black women is essential to understanding how and why healthcare inequities occur. The remainder of this chapter provides a framework for understanding how stereotypes, including specific stereotypes of Black women, affect Black women's health and healthcare.

As I argue throughout this chapter, healthcare settings may be characterized as a "White space" through which Black middle-class women must navigate. To survive in predominantly White institutions (e.g., work, school, etc.) that comprise the "White space," many middle-class Black Americans swallow numerous indignities. They may modify their clothing, their comportment, and their speech, all in an effort to mitigate how they are judged and received in these White spaces (Anderson, 2015; Malat, van Ryn, & Purcell, 2006; Sacks, 2017).

Similar to the women in this study, scholars, journalists, and pundits have described the need to manage one's impression to fit into overwhelmingly White, cis-hetero-normative, able- bodied, upper middle-class, and Judeo-Christian environments. Sociologist Irving Goffman coined the phrase "impression management," or positive self-presentation, to describe the ways in which people purposefully manage their persona to manipulate or control the outcome of social interaction (1959). Goffman described the intuitive, human effort to put one's best foot forward in social situations (e.g., with a potential mate or employer). Although Goffman does not explicitly address how self-presentation interacts with race, gender, class, or other categories, one may assume he was laying out a universal theory of social behavior.

However, because Black Americans occupy a precarious position in American society, Black impression management has always been more complicated. Black people have been subject to racist and sexist subordination, overt discrimination, and rampant stereotyping (Kwate & Meyer, 2011). With pervasive stereotyping and discrimination ever present, Black people have adapted by being vigilant to social cues and adopting certain cultural mores around grooming, style of dress, hair, and speech. Black people often feel the need to manage their self-presentation by behaving and appearing in ways that are socially acceptable to Whites (Lee & Hicken, 2016).

For example, in psychologist Claude Steele's work on stereotype threat, he recounts a story about a Black graduate student (Steele, 2011). Although the young man was an accomplished student, the White people he encountered daily seemed afraid of him. White women feared being mugged and crossed the street to avoid him. People in elevators with him were frequently anxious, which in turn caused him great frustration and distress. The stereotype of the threatening, criminal Black man pursued him as doggedly as he pursued his own education. To adapt to the constant stress caused by these daily insults, the young man conjured up his own strategy. In an elevator with a group of White people he decided to whistle a tune by the classical music composer Vivaldi. He observed his elevator-mates visible relief that, by virtue of knowing classical music, he was transformed into a palatable, safe student and not the Black criminal of their imagination[2] (Steele, 2011).

This, and other observations from his own life, led Steele to consider how stereotyping often constrains and stifles Black people in their day-to-day lives. The concept of stereotype- threat contends that members of targeted groups (like ethno-racial minorities, women, sexual minorities, etc.) are acutely aware of how they are perceived by the dominant society. Women know they are stereotyped as less competent than men in mathematic ability. Black people know they are believed to be less intelligent than White people. In empirical tests, Steele demonstrated that this awareness led members of the target group to change their behavior, which led to poorer performance. For example, in an experiment designed to test the effect of stereotype threat on academic performance, Black students who were told they were being evaluated on their intellectual capacity performed worse than when they took the same tests but were not told it was an evaluation of their intellectual capacity overall. In other words, priming Black students to perform intellectual tasks for which they knew they were stereotyped as intellectually inferior actually lowered their performance. The

---

[2] My discussion of stereotype threat should not be taken as an endorsement of the idea that people should have to signal their humanity to White people to be treated with the dignity and respect. Rather, my argument is a critique of the enormous burden this adjustment requires.

activation of the stereotype made it difficult for them to perform to their highest capability. And, importantly, these stereotypes are levied at, and may potentially damage, the target regardless of class status.

Steele later found stereotype threat was a powerful determinant of behavior and outcomes in both educational and workplace settings (1997). Later, one of his graduate students, Joshua Aronson, now a distinguished professor in his own right, applied the idea of stereotype threat to the study of healthcare settings. Health-related stereotype threat posits that even in doctor's offices, clinics, or hospitals, patients recognize the threat of being stereotyped (Aronson, Burgess, Phelan, & Juarez, 2013). Aronson and other colleagues describe health-related stereotype threat as elements of the clinical encounter that trigger a sense of unease for minority patients in which they recognize that they may be stereo-typed as being a waste of provider's time: unintelligent, unworthy of quality care, unable to adhere to medical protocols, or generally unpleasant (Burgess, Warren, Phelan, Dovidio, & van Ryn, 2010). Patients may believe that they are viewed as second-class citizens and may change their behavior as a result (Aronson et al., 2013). They may be unable to pay attention to what the doctor says or may dis-regard their advice altogether. Importantly, the idea of health-related stereotype threat contends that patients may experience increased anxiety and emotional arousal, difficulty processing or discounting treatment information, and disen-gagement from treatment (Burgess et al., 2010). Last, Aronson and colleagues note that the healthcare environment may be threatening to patients regardless of how the provider interacts with them. In other words, the emotional and physical consequences of the threat may still affect people even if the provider treats them well or appears unbiased. This suggests that focusing all of our inter-ventions at the level of patient–provider may not be sufficient to override the stereotyping and racism that is pervasive in American society.

Other studies have explored the extent to which Black people, including the Black middle class, and other minorities try to manipulate the way they pres-ent themselves in healthcare settings to try to mitigate negative or biased treat-ment (Malat et al., 2006). Malat and colleagues describe a situation in which an African American physician brings her young daughter to the emergency department. When the emergency physician provides a cursory examination of the child and tells the mother to take her home, the African American physician and mother responds by using sophisticated medical terminology. Eventually, the emergency physician's demeanor changes, she calls the attending physician, and the child is determined to have pneumonia. This vignette illustrates the cultural health capital resources African Americans may call upon to minimize differences in treatment (Dubbin, Chang, & Shim, 2013). In this case, it took emphasizing professional medical expertise to get the proper level of care.

While many people feel the need to emphasize their knowledge or compe-
tencies during an interaction with a physician, Black people may be more likely
to do so because, as stereotype threat contends, they are assumed to be less
intelligent or less competent compared to their White counterparts. As a result,
feeling as though one has to put one's best foot forward may be more salient to
African Africans compared to other people for whom negative stereotyping is
less pervasive.

To test this hypothesis empirically, Malat and colleagues (2006) conducted a telephone survey of almost 700 Whites and 500 African Americans
in Cincinnati, Ohio. Respondents were queried about whether they tried
to get the best treatment possible by wearing nice clothing to the doctor,
showing that they were intelligent, demonstrating that they were concerned
about their health, and the like. The authors hypothesized that African
Americans and lower income groups would be acutely aware of the stereotypes they face and would adopt these strategies to minimize negative treatment. They found that African Americans and lower income persons were
more likely than the Whites and higher income groups to agree that wearing
nice clothes, using big words, and other forms of cultural health capital were
an important component of how one should behave at the doctor's office.
Other groups who are often the targets of stereotypes, such as women and
older people, were also more likely to view these adaptations as more important compared to men and younger people. Furthermore, the Black people
in the sample were more likely than the White people to agree that manipu-
lating one's self-presentation was important even after controlling for socioeconomic status.

The implications of these studies are significant. First, they confirm the
idea that stereotyping, which necessarily affects people regardless of their
class status, can affect individual behavior and physiological functioning.
Second, taking this finding a step further, the studies suggest that the perception of stereotyping can have a profound effect on human health and
well-being. Ultimately, it may help us understand health inequities, particularly for the Black middle class who are not burdened by poverty but are
often in predominantly White environments (i.e., work, school, healthcare
settings, etc.). The process of stereotyping, and the adjustments people feel
they must make to mitigate it, may negatively affect Black people's health
through stress, misdiagnosis, or delayed treatment. Last, these studies document the painful indignities and adjustments Black people endure just to get
through the day.

Stereotyping and Its Health Effects

Many public health scholars have empirically documented that racism and stereotyping are stressors that lead to a host of physical and mental health problems including bio-psycho-social stress (Blascovich, Spencer, Quinn, & Steele, 2001; Clark, Anderson, Clark, & Williams, 1999; Harrell, Hall, & Taliaferro, 2003), premature aging (see weathering hypothesis; Geronimus et al., 2010), and stresses to the body's regulatory system, also called *allostatic load* (Krieger, 2001a; McEwen & Seeman, 1999). For example, McEwan and Seeman found that chronic stress is a constant, as opposed to intermittent, form of physiological wear and tear that leads to high allostatic load and, ultimately, disease. Some scholars suggest that the strain associated with discrimination increases allostatic load, which may ultimately explain the persistence of health disparities among the Black middle class (Krieger, 2001a). In other words, echoing Ruth Gilmore's definition of racism, discrimination and stress may tax the body to the point of premature death (2007).

In an effort to cope with these persistent challenges, many Black people, especially the Black middle class, have adopted what some scholars have termed "the politics of respectability," or the idea that one must behave and look a certain way to avoid negative treatment and be treated with respect. In fact, sociologists Hedwig Lee and Margaret Takako Hicken recently tested the impact of respectability politics on Black people's health (2016). They noted that Black people believe they must shield themselves from daily slights, prejudice, and overt discrimination (2016). To do so, Black people employ what Lee and Hicken term, a "vigilant coping style" in which they actively manage their impression to the outside world. Similar to the Malat study, Lee and Hicken note that this may include being particularly careful about their physical appearance and clothing, the way they speak, or by simply avoiding social situations and places where they anticipate experiencing discrimination. For example, as 55-year-old study respondent Bella remarked, even getting dressed for a doctor's appointment requires forethought:

> You can have on jeans and a top, but as long as you're nice and neat and you present yourself, you know, like you care about yourself, I think that's important. 'Cause I think they will treat you the way you go in; they'll treat you the way you look. That's not to say all doctors do that, but the majority of them are.

Bella recognizes that the performance of self does not stop simply because one is under the weather. Instead, even in a healthcare setting Black women, yet again, must contend with how their appearance affects how they are treated. This coping style is also characterized by "anticipatory and ruminative thoughts and behaviors involved in the preparation for discriminatory treatment" (p. 425). In lay terms, Lee and Hicken suggest that because racial discrimination is so pervasive, Black people are often waiting for the other shoe to drop, and, as much of the research bears out, it often does.

But how does this affect health? The empirical research suggests that anticipating prejudice or discrimination may activate biological stress response systems even more than other types of stress (Sawyer, Major, Casad, Townsend, & Mendes, 2012). Also, because interpersonal, vicarious, and structural discrimination are common in the United States, these forms of stress become chronic, which negatively affects well-being as whole. As stated earlier, many scholars have documented the relationship between chronic race-related stress and poorer health outcomes, such as differences in stress-related biological aging, hypertension, and exposure to environmental toxins, among others (Geronimus et al., 2010; Hicken, Gragg et al., 2011; Sternthal, Slopen et al., 2011; Turner, 2009). However, unlike previous research, Lee and Hickens were able to demonstrate the specific connection between engaging in impression management or "respectability politics" and poorer health outcomes. In their study of Black people in Chicago, Lee and Hickens found that both Black men and women reported engaging in "vigilant behavior," including preparing for possible insults before leaving home, being very careful about their appearance, and carefully watching what they said and how they said it. Furthermore, they found that engaging in vigilant behavior was associated with poorer physical and mental health (as measured through chronic health conditions, depressive symptoms, and self-rated health) (Lee & Hicken, 2016).

The results of these studies cannot be overstated. They document the physiological toll that racism and discrimination takes on Black people, including those who are not poor. They also indicate that because Black people are aware of their position in society, they enact certain compensatory strategies to mitigate stereotyping and discrimination. However, these strategies come at a heavy emotional, psychological, and physiological price.

Given this backdrop, understanding the characteristics of the Black middle class, particularly Black middle-class women, and the stereotypes they face is a critical step toward understanding why differences in treatment occur, how they affect women's health, and, ultimately, what we can do to stop them. The remainder of this chapter leads us toward this charge by (1) analyzing specific stereotypes that Black women face and (2) providing an analytical framework from which to understand health disparities among Black middle-class women.

Poverty, Race and Gender: How All Black People Became "Poor" and All Black Women Became "Welfare Queens"

Focusing exclusively on poor Black people obscures the extent to which health disparities can be attributed to structural racism (and other forms of discrimination) in addition to poverty. In other words, because the preponderance of research about Black people is done on *poor* Black people, negative outcomes are easily explained away by poverty without acknowledging the impact of racism. For example, because being poor is certainly bad for one's health, Black people's health status may be understood as a function of material deprivation without considering the specific effects of racism. Furthermore, our focus on the Black poor necessarily limits the scope of what we can possibly know about the totality of the Black experience, especially intraracial variation in life experience based on class.

Furthermore, while we have come to accept the focus on Black poverty (and the negative outcomes with which it is associated), political scientist Martin Gilens argues that the fact Black people have almost become synonymous with poverty is not accidental. Gilens notes that in the early twentieth century, the face of American poverty was overwhelmingly White and rural. Images of deprived White families in Appalachia were common and certainly more common than Black families in urban ghettos. In fact, as Gilens argues, although Black people were always disproportionately represented among the ranks of the American poor, their suffering was largely invisible (2003).

However, by the mid-twentieth century, a perfect storm of social changes, including the Great Migration (in which approximately 6 million Black people left the rural South for urban centers in the North) and the Civil Rights movement, made Black life and Black suffering more apparent to the majority of the country. Although this demographic shift made Black poverty visible, it did not elicit the same sympathy afforded to poor Appalachian Whites. While the White poor were viewed with wary compassion, Black people were viewed with contempt and suspicion that they were living off the dole and unwilling to work. Of course, in the 1980s Ronald Reagan exploited the stereotype of the lazy, cheating Black woman on welfare (i.e., the "welfare queen") to great effect (Gilens, 1998; Gustafson, 2009; Hancock, 2004).

Returning to sociologist Anderson's work on the tendency to conflate poverty and Blackness (Anderson, 2015; Anderson et al., 2012), he notes that Black poverty, stigma, and pathology have converged into an icon of destitution and crime, which he labels the "iconic ghetto." Anderson argues that the iconic ghetto has come to represent all Black people in the White imaginary. As a result, in spite of the post-Civil Rights economic and social gains of the Black middle class, Black people are still thought to be poor, pathological, and living in an iconic ghetto. Furthermore, Anderson argues that, because Blacks are viewed through the prism of the iconic ghetto, any venture into what is perceived as the "White space" (i.e., a space overwhelmingly occupied by Whites) may be met with hostility or derision.

Although Anderson does not explicitly count healthcare among the institutional settings that could be characterized as "White space" (e.g., workplaces, public space, schools, recreational settings, etc.), I would argue American healthcare institutions are such spaces. For example, in 2013, out of all active physicians in the United States, only 4.1% were Black (Conrad et al., 2014). Of that small percentage of Black physicians, almost 55% were Black women. However, the dearth of Black physicians may be used as a proxy to suggest that the majority of Black people receive healthcare in predominately non-Black settings. In other words, like most other American institutions, American healthcare could be characterized as a "White space" in which Black people are thought to be marginal and less credible than White people.

Christina, a 43-year-old study respondent described an experience in which her credibility was overtly questioned. During our interview, she recalled an incident at her son's orthodontist in downtown Chicago. She described waiting in the car for her son to get his braces tightened when, after an unusually short time, he returned,

> . . . crying and upset. And I said, "what's wrong?" And he said, "They said you didn't pay the bill and they won't let me." I said, "What they mean I didn't pay the bill? I paid the bill off! What are you talking about? I don't owe them nothing."

Irritated that the receptionist had spoken harshly to her son, Christina went to find out what happened:

> So I went upstairs and the lady said they didn't treat him bad. I said, "You told my son that I didn't pay the bill. I need you to look up this bill." I had my phone and I went online and I said, "This bill was paid, I've got the check number here. We don't owe anything." So they look it up and they found it and they said, "We're so, so sorry." I said, "You should have just looked it up the first time, but you didn't do that, you just assumed."

Christina was obviously frustrated at the presumption that she had not paid her bill and that she had not been given the benefit of the doubt. As if exemplifying the tenets of Anderson's "White space," Christina's orthodontist was in a predominantly White and exclusive area of downtown Chicago. However, it is important to note that her son's orthodontist was a Black man. As psychiatrist and social scientist Jonathon Metzl's cautions, simply increasing the proportion of Black providers alone may not reduce the stress caused by racial bias or the subsequent racial inequities it may produce (Metzl & Hansen, 2014). Christina and her son were not given the benefit of the doubt and faced additional scrutiny from the allied staff even though the orthodontist was also Black.

As Christina's experience illustrates, any effort to understand the causes of health inequities must grapple with the implications of pervasive stereotyping, particularly with regard to the ways Black people have been lumped into the category of the shiftless, lazy poor.[3] I must make clear that I am not suggesting that social scientists forego studying poor Black people or that we should not do everything we can to reduce poverty. Nor do I intend to pathologize poor Black people while lauding Black middle-class mores and respectability. Rather, I am critiquing the fact that the stereotype of the Black poor ensnares all Black people, including the Black middle class who may nonetheless try to differentiate themselves from poorer Black people. As such, in keeping with Kwate and Meyer, I argue that stereotyping is a mechanism of racist subordination that operates at both the structural and individual levels (2011). Furthermore, efforts to differentiate oneself from poorer Black people should be interpreted through a structural framework, not simply as an enactment of respectability politics or shaming of the poor.[4] As I argue throughout the book, stereotyping and its effect on the Black middle class is a crucial and underexplored determinant of Black women's health.

The Intersection of Race and Gender: Stereotypes and Black Women

While much of the research on stereotyping and the Black experience centers Black men, Black feminist scholars have focused on how Black women live at the intersection of race and gender. Black feminist theorists including Patricia Hill Collins, Melissa Harris-Perry, and others delineate the most pervasive and damaging stereotypes that affect Black women. In her Black feminist manifesto, Collins argues that stereotypes of Black women are used to control the

---

[3] The lack of empathy for the poor in the United States is well-documented (Gilens, 1998; 2009) and beyond the scope of this book. In addition, other scholars have pointed out that, in addition to antipathy for the poor in general, Americans demonstrate a lack of empathy for different racial groups and people whom they perceive to be fundamentally different from themselves (Cikara, Bruneau, Van Bavel, & Saxe, 2014).

[4] People may have their own rationale for enacting certain behaviors. However, I argue that even these interpretations may be understood at both the individual and structural levels of analysis.

ideological landscape against which they are judged. In Collin's estimation, stereotypes of Black women, which she calls "controlling images," are used to mute
Black women's critique of racism, sexism, poverty, heterosexism, and more. In
this manner, stereotypes become normalized and inevitable parts of everyday
life (Collins, 2000). Collins notes,

> Within US culture, racist and sexist ideologies permeate the social
> structure to such a degree that they become hegemonic, namely, seen as
> natural, normal, and inevitable. In this context, certain assumed quali-
> ties that are attached to Black women are used to justify oppression.
> From the mammies, jezebels, and breeder women of slavery to the smil-
> ing Aunt Jemimas on pancake mix boxes, ubiquitous Black prostitutes,
> and ever-present welfare mothers of contemporary popular culture,
> negative stereotypes applied to African-American women have been
> fundamental to Black women's oppression. (2000, p. 7)

Given the organic quality of racist and sexist (classist, heterosexist, etc.)
norms in American life, Collins's indictment is particularly relevant to the
healthcare encounter. One need not be racist, prejudiced, male, female, White,
or Black to hold negative stereotypes of Black people because these controlling
images are so pervasive, normalized, and often beyond the level of conscious
awareness.

While Collins explicates the naturalness of controlling images/stereotypes of
Black women, Harris-Perry argues that Black women's lives are inherently political because they must consistently resist particular derogatory assumptions
about their character and identity.

Grounded in theories of political participation and political philosophy,
Harris-Perry outlines three recurring characterizations of black women: the
Jezebel, the hypersexual, predatory black woman; the Mammy, the heavy-set,
asexual domestic worker who happily serves her White charges at the expense of
her own family; and the Sapphire, the angry, emasculating, wise-cracking "sista"
(Harris-Perry, 2011). There are many corollaries to these stereotypes, including the "welfare queen," the black woman who does not control her fertility, has
children with multiple partners, and subsequently relies on the state to support
them (Gilens, 2009).

Harris-Perry uses these frames to analyze how stereotyping forces women to
adjust their behavior and fight for recognition in the American polity. Harris-
Perry argues that women both resist and accommodate stereotypes depending on the situation. In all cases, however, resisting the stereotypes necessitates
additional "work" in which women try to mold themselves either into or away
from the pervasive controlling images to which they are subjected. Given that

these stereotypes float in the ether, often beyond our conscious awareness, it follows that they affect encounters between healthcare providers and patients. As a result, Black women may feel they must resist these negative characterizations, which in turn necessitates a behavioral adjustment. To better understand what Black women are up against from the moment they walk through a provider's door, the specific manifestations of these stereotypes will be described briefly here.

The Jezebel: Hypersexuality and Promiscuity

Portrayals of Black women as "hoochies," "hot mammas," or as hypersexual women of suspect moral character is one of the most common stereotypes of Black women as a whole.

The origins of this stereotype trace back to slavery, in which Black women's supposed hypersexual nature was used to justify their sexual victimization at the hands of White male slave owners. In an era in which Black women were often forced to bear children by their slave owners, thereby creating more slaves and more free labor, the perpetuation of the hypsersexual Black woman myth supported political, economic, and social goals.

While White society used stereotypes of Black women to perpetuate the economic and social order, African Americans readily adopted many of these negative characterizations as well (Collins, 2000; Harris-Perry, 2011). According to Harris-Perry,

> While the myth of black women's hypersexuality may have been historically created and perpetuated by hite social, political, and economic institutions, its contemporary manifestations are often seen just as clearly in the internal politics of African American communities. (2011 p. 55)

Given that, within their own communities and in their interactions with the dominant society, Black women were often considered lewd and generally disreputable, they had to carve out some semblance of a tolerable, respectable self-concept. In an effort to uphold middle-class values and to counter such widely held views of their womanhood, Black women in public life shunned any hint of sexuality, make-up, or any public romantic relationships (Harris-Perry, 2011). However, their efforts to live modestly, control their fertility, and form lasting relationships occurred in the context of extreme degradation of their character and legitimate threats to their physical safety.

The Mammy: Asexuality and Self-Sacrifice

After slavery ended and Black women were no longer needed to reproduce more slaves, a new stereotype of Black womanhood was necessary to explain Black women's shifting domestic role in the homes of White people. The sexual seductress could not be allowed to work in a respectable White home, raise White children, and have any proximity to White men. As a result, Black women were reimagined as asexual, corpulent, omni-competent, devoted servants. Jezebel, however, did not disappear. Rather, Mammy came to represent another type of Black woman, one who was acceptable to work in genteel White domesticity.

To fit neatly into White households and the public imagination, Black women were recast as having no individual needs of their own. In contrast to Jezebel, Mammy had no sexual desires. She was docile and maternal, and, perhaps most importantly, fat, dark-skinned, and unfeminine. She also gladly subordinated the needs of her own children and family to those of her White employer. In this manner, Mammy became a palatable counternarrative to the exotic Jezebel while simultaneously inviting derision from the Black community for betraying her own (Harris-Perry, 2011).

The Sapphire: Emasculating and Aggressive

Although the myths of the Jezebel and the Mammy originated around the antebellum and Reconstruction eras, the angry Black woman is a relatively more recent phenomenon. This stereotype reportedly began with the portrayal of the nagging, assertive Sapphire character on the 1930s "Amos 'n Andy" radio show. Over time, the angry Black woman has taken on slightly different manifestations including the brash, independent, hostile Black woman, the Black "bitch," and the emasculating matriarch (Harris-Perry, 2011). According to Black feminist writers Marcyliena Morgan and Dionne Bennett,

> The stereotype of the angry, mean Black woman goes unnamed not because it is insignificant, but because it is considered an essential characteristic of Black femininity regardless of the other stereotypical roles a Black woman may be accused of occupying. These stereotypes are more than representations; they are representations that shape realities. (quoted in Harris-Perry, 2011, p. 89)

Judging from Black women's self-report in the few research studies that have explored Black women's self-concept, there is evidence to suggest that these stereotypes indeed shape Black women's perceptions, particularly of how they think others see them. In focus groups conducted for her study of the effect of stereotyping on political participation, Harris-Perry found that when Black women were asked how others would describe them, they often said sassy, mouthy, attitude, aggressive, go-getter, self-starter, smart-ass, stubborn, crazy, moody, and the like (2011). This was in contrast to how they described themselves, which included being gentle, thoughtful, and kind.

Psychologists Jones and Shorter-Gooden also found that Black women reported feeling pressured to calibrate their assertiveness and minimize their accomplishments to make everyone more comfortable (2003).

The angry Black woman stereotype is particularly binding because it invalidates the legitimate expression of frustration or resistance to structural oppression. For example, Black women cannot critique Black men's misogynoir because that is tantamount to betraying the race. One must demonstrate racial solidarity regardless of the sexism Black women face in their communities. As a result, many Black women try to suppress feelings of bitterness or rage, whether directed at the dominant society or intraracially, to avoid being transformed into Sapphire (Yarbrough & Bennett, 1999).

The Jezebel, Mammy, and Sapphire stereotypes paint a false picture of Black women as two-dimensional caricatures, not individuals (Yarbrough & Bennett, 1999). Moreover, being stripped of an individual identity leads to the misrecognition of one's humanity, authenticity, and personhood. The overwhelmingly negative characteristics of these stereotypes also lead to stigma and shame. As a result, many theorists, including Cathy Cohen and Harris-Perry, describe the stigmatizing shame Black women face, which is levied against all members of a group that share this identity. Harris-Perry notes,

> Stigmatizing shame such as that deployed against African Americans affects not only those who directly encounter the social rejection but the entire class of citizens who share an identity trait. There is no possibility of accurate, democratic recognition of citizens who are subjected to stigmatizing shame. Racism functions by stereotyping all members of a group based on a set of assumed negative characteristics. This means that the shaming experiences of the welfare office affect not only the poor mother who encounters them directly but all African American women regardless of social class or marital or parental status. (2010, p. 116)

The Strong Black Woman (aka Superwoman)

In contrast to the pejorative connotations of the aforementioned stereotypes, the strong Black woman, also sometimes referred to as the "superwoman ideal," may have emerged to counter these negative frames. The strong Black woman role is characterized by caretaking, independence, restricted emotionality, and economic self-reliance (Nelson, Cardemil, & Adeoye, 2016). Because these traits are thought to be positive in American society, some theorists have suggested that the strong Black woman ideal emerged to counter the overwhelmingly negative portrayals of Black women in American culture (Beauboeuf- Lafontant, 2005; Collins, 2000; Harris-Perry, 2011). For example, emotional self-regulation and financial independence are exact opposites of the traits associated with the angry Black woman and the welfare queen. Moreover, the strong Black woman is often internalized by Black women and upheld by the Black community in general.

Although many Black women may actively support the idea that they can overcome any obstacle with emotional control, hard work, and perseverance, similar to the concept of John Henryism, no amount of emotional regulation or independence can overcome the structural barriers Black women face. In fact, several scholars have begun to investigate the relationship between embracing the superwoman ideal and poor health outcomes among Black women in particular (Nelson et al., 2002; Nuru-Jeter et al., 2009). Although this research is nascent, it suggests that, like the other adaptations Black people have made to overcome discrimination, being a "strong Black woman" may contribute to physiological wear and tear.

Taken together, stereotypes, particularly those that are levied at Black women, are part of an ideological landscape that negatively affects the day-to-day lives of Black people. From the "White space" to being mistaken for not paying your child's orthodontist bill, stereotypes affect all members of a group regardless of class status. As political scientist Cathy Cohen and sociologist Karyn Lacy observe in their in-depth explorations of intraracial class dynamics, being middle class and Black does not buy you out of discrimination or guard against stereotyping. The following section analyzes their work and provides an analytical foundation for the remainder of this book.

Theoretical Approaches to Studying the Black Middle Class

The work of political scientist Cathy Cohen and sociologists Karyn Lacy and Mary Pattillo has pushed the boundaries of how we understand the Black middle class as well as the intraracial class dynamics in the Black community. Cohen, Lacy, and Pattillo are unusual in that they depart from social science methodological conventions by focusing solely on Black people alone, not in comparison to White people. Rather, they focus their scholarly endeavors on understanding political, social, and economic differences within the Black community. Specifically, Cohen's critique of the Black community's response to the

HIV/AIDS crisis, *Boundaries of Blackness: AIDS and the Breakdown of Black Politics* (1999), is an important example of scholarship that addresses political complexities and social stratification among African Americans. Furthermore, Lacy's work on middle class Blacks in the Washington, DC, suburbs, *Blue-Chip Black* (2007), hypothesizes that middle-class Black people work hard to differentiate themselves from poorer Black people and use their class status to navigate through predominately White spaces like their neighborhoods, schools, workplaces, and the like. Pattillo's seminal work in *Black Picket Fences* (2013) provides a rich description of the lives of African Americans in a lower middle-class neighborhood of Chicago and provides empirical evidence of the tenuousness and vulnerability of Black people who are middle class but nonetheless face economic and social precariousness. *Boundaries of Blackness, Blue-Chip Black,* and *Black Picket Fences* explicitly draw attention to the power dynamics within Black communities and provide the theoretical foundation from which to study the uses and limitations of this power. In this manner, these scholars excavate the tensions between ideological solidarity and increasing within-group divisions. Furthermore, these scholars problematize the idea that all Black people share the same political and social interests, as well as the notion that they are uniformly powerless relative to majority society.

Cohen notes that while African Americans have less power relative to members of the dominant society, they employ their own sources of power to shape public discourse and political action within the Black community. Although Cohen acknowledges the complexity of power relations in the Black community, her work hinges on the notion that African Americans remain a marginal group, which she defines as "those, who, to varying degrees, exist politically, socially, or economically 'outside' of dominant norms and institutions" (p. 37). Furthermore, Cohen theorizes that African Americans have a stigmatized or illegitimate social identity that is considered abhorrent by the dominant society. Cohen explains:

> The stigmatization of an identity results from a process of social construction that defines certain behaviors, beliefs, or physical characteristics as abnormal and deficient. Marginal groups exist within a societal framework in which one or more of their primary identities have come to signal inherent inferiority.
>
> Dominant, even indigenous, ideologies, institutions, and social relationships are used to create and maintain the definition of marginal groups as "other." Consequently, through the process of marginalization, a group's stigmatized identity works to constrain the opportunities and rights afforded community members, helping to solidify their secondary status. (Cohen, 1999, p. 38)

In addition to the stigma associated with Black women's identities, Cohen notes that ideological beliefs are a necessary component of power, domination, and resistance. As such, ideology represents a necessary component of marginalization. Ideology refers to the "systems of beliefs that frame and guide our general understanding of, and interaction in, the world" (Cohen, 1999, p. 41). Ideology provides a normative framework through which we evaluate what is deviant and what is not. Because ideological beliefs are directly related to norms and values, they "confer legitimacy and authority and thus are directly tied to the distribution of power in society" (p. 41).

Thus, dominant ideological frameworks permeate the context in which women navigate the White space of healthcare. Cohen's work, along with other scholars such as Kimberle Crenshaw and Patricia Hill Collins, acknowledges the multiple forms of oppression people face based on gender, race, class, sexual orientation, and more. This body of work, called *intersectionality*, integrates women's struggle against sexism, racism, classism, and other forms of discrimination. Acknowledging the interplay of these elements allows for a more fluid analysis of women's efforts to resist oppression (Collins, 2000; Crenshaw, 1991; Samuels and Ross-Sheriff, 2008). It is therefore an important framework for understanding how Black women negotiate social contexts in which they are simultaneously powerful and marginalized.

In contrast to Cohen, Lacy's research explores the extent to which middle-class African Americans strategically manipulate their identity and public personas to mitigate discrimination. The families Lacy describes in *Blue-Chip Black* emphasize the importance of constructing a uniquely Black and middle-class identity for themselves and their children, expending extensive energy differentiating themselves from the White middle class, the Black poor, and the Black lower middle class (2007). Lacy's critique of some of the seminal work on the Black middle class conducted by Feagin and Sikes in *Living with Racism* (1994) is that it downplays the arsenal of resources middle-class Black people have to manage discriminatory treatment. Lacy suggests professional Black people use cultural resources to manage their interactions with Whites, although she omits an analysis of the extent to which they feel the need to use these cultural resources with other Black people.

In *Blue-Chip Black*, Lacy argues that all segments of the Black middle class, but particularly those with well above $50,000 per year, cultivate a constellation of behaviors, or *cultural capital*, including language, mannerisms, clothing, and credentials, to develop a way of carrying themselves while in public, which Lacy terms a "public identity." These public identities are used strategically to reduce or avert potential discriminatory treatment. As Lacy writes:

The experiences of middle class blacks in my study suggest that those who actively correct the misapprehensions of White strangers reduce the likelihood of discriminatory treatment. This invocation of a public identity is a deliberate, conscious act—one that entails psychological costs as well as rewards. (2007, p. 48)

The psychological costs to which Lacy refers harkens back to W. E. B. DuBois's concept of "double consciousness" that requires a type of psychological splitting into two separate worlds: one Black and the other White. "The continual enactment of a public self," Lacy writes, "can be exhausting, and the perceived need to don a public identity that accurately telegraphs class status in order to secure smooth transactions in the White world can be infuriating" (p. 45).

In Lacy's argument, middle-class Blacks with high household incomes (>$100,000k/year) differentiate themselves from lower and lower middle-class Blacks through exclusionary boundary work in which they distance themselves from poorer Black people while simultaneously trying to emphasize areas of consensus and shared experience with middle-class White people. The people in Lacy's study also consciously telegraphed their class status in public settings through improvisational processes and script-switching. Developed as an adaptation to experiences in a racialized society, these informal strategies ultimately culminate in the development of an identity that is both African American and middle class.

Because so much research about Black people centers on the poor, scholars like Cohen, Lacy, Pattillo, and others represent a very important contribution to within-group research on class and race. However, while Cohen critiques the Black community's emphasis on respectability and class status, *Blue-Chip Black* risks reifying class divisions in describing the behavior and values of the Black middle class. Lacy does not comment on the possibility that while boundary work is an adaptive feature of the Black middle class, it may also reinforce the politics of respectability and disdain for poor Black people.

In sum, the work of Cohen, Lacy, Pattillo, and other seminal scholars of the Black middle class lays the foundation for emerging scholarship that analyzes intraracial class variation and the relationship between race and class for Black people who are not poor. Furthermore, the conceptual contributions of Steele, Anderson, Crenshaw, Harris-Perry, and others highlight the overwhelming importance of stereotyping as a social determinant of health, including for Black middle-class women. Other scholars have found empirical support for the idea that the behavioral adaptations people make to stereotyping (e.g., wearing certain clothes or emphasizing their intelligence or career) have negative health consequences. Taken together, these bodies of research illuminate the stories of the women who appear in the following pages.

2

Invisible Visits

Black Middle-Class Women in the American Healthcare System

> Negros, regardless of their affluence or respectability, wear the badge of color.
>
> —St. Clair Drake and Horace Cayton, *Black Metropolis: A Study of Negro Life in a Northern City* (1945)

> I've noticed situations, and maybe in my own mind I try to avoid being stereotyped by doing certain things. I don't know what may be in someone's mind, but I just really think that sometimes how you present yourself, how you speak, how you're dressed, sometimes plays into—unfortunately, that plays into the quality of care that you may receive—and that's from the time you walk in all the way up to the time that you see the doctor.
>
> —Leona, 59, executive director of dance company

On a typically raw Chicago evening in January 2011, I headed north from my home on the Southside to meet Leona, a 59-year-old woman who had agreed to tell me her story about dealing with doctors. Leona lived in a gleaming downtown high-rise with revolving doors that guarded its residents from the whistling lakefront winds Chicagoans refer to as the "hawk." At almost 60 years of age, her silky face was remarkably beautiful and she later told me she had been the first Black woman to win a beauty pageant called Ms. Wheelchair America. Leona graciously welcomed me into her condo, which was small and tastefully decorated with black-and-white photos of her extended family strategically arranged on the walls.

As we exchanged pleasantries, Leona recalled a life in pursuit of education and art.

Although she contracted polio when she was only five years old, Leona excelled at school and persevered through multiple surgeries to mitigate her postpolio paralysis. In spite of her disability, she had traveled extensively and made a living as an actor, dancer, and vocalist.

In her early 20s, Leona completed her college education, married, and had a son who was now finishing his medical residency at a prestigious university. Although she recently separated from her husband, Leona fulfilled a lifelong dream of starting a nonprofit agency to allow disabled and abled dancers to share the stage. She served as the executive director of the nonprofit and lived on its modest salary and spousal support from her husband.

Even before the formal interview began, Leona spoke freely about her overall impression of the healthcare system, particularly healthcare providers. She intimated that her identity as a Black, female, disabled older adult indelibly shaped the care she received. Perhaps even more striking was Leona's characterization of how her perception of stereotyping affected her from the moment she entered the room. She described the need to "let them know I'm on top of my health and to try to interact with people so that they know that." She noted that this was just part of what "we have to do to make people at ease with us." Leona did not explicitly describe what she meant by "us" although I interpreted her remarks to be about her identity as a Black woman who is also disabled. Leona later described the uncertainty she faced in healthcare settings: "I don't know if that's a class issue, a race issue, a disability issue, but I just always try to make sure that whoever I'm seeing knows that I'm not just a run-of-the-mill person that doesn't understand things well."

Leona's experience, along with most of the 30 women who participated in focus groups or interviews for this study, presents a different narrative from what is commonly seen in social science research and popular culture. In other words, she is female and Black but not poor. This chapter takes up stories of women like Leona, who feel they must use their class and cultural resources to manage the racial and gender discrimination they anticipate in healthcare settings. As I argue throughout the book, women use these resources, to which some sociologists refer as *self-presentation strategies* or forms of cultural health capital, to resist persistent race and gender discrimination. Although the women I interviewed ranged from lower middle to upper middle class, their experience of the healthcare system was quite similar, suggesting that race and gender trumped their socioeconomic status (SES) and the interpersonal skills they had accrued throughout their lives. They may have been able to emphasize their education, their ability to research medical problems, or their winning personalities, but these skills were not enough to overcome the nagging stereotypes Black women face at the doctor. The women tried to use all the charm and skill possible to win the provider over, and, while some felt they were successful in doing so, most were not so sure.

Although one might expect middle-class women to view the healthcare system with less apprehension than poor women, the women I interviewed seemed to anticipate discrimination regardless of their class status. This suggests that SES alone is insufficient to erase pervasive negative anti-Black misogyny, often referred to as *misogynoir* (Hobson, 2016). Women noted that these often-invisible barriers left them feeling burdened by the constant need to perform or fight for legitimacy. In fact, Leona noted that she expended significant effort to get healthcare professionals to see that she is not just a "run of the mill person." In other words, she worked hard to play against whatever implicit or explicit stereotypes physicians may have held about Black women.

Another woman I interviewed, Christina, was 43 years old and grew up poor on Chicago's Southside. I interviewed her at the three-story building she owned in a neighborhood near the University of Chicago. She operated a home daycare business out of the same space, and, during the interview, she left her young charges in the care of a younger female assistant. Unlike Leona, Christina came across as no-nonsense, kind but slightly gruff, and perhaps a little world-weary. When she answered her door, she didn't smile or give me much energy. She simply stepped to the side and ushered me in. Her demeanor didn't surprise me as I figured the Southside of Christina's youth had demanded a certain carriage. You couldn't be weak in the gritty Chi-town of the '70s and '80s, and Christina certainly seemed like she could've managed just fine. On the day of the interview, she was dressed casually in jeans and a T-shirt. Her short hair was arranged in little spikes framing dark skin dappled with acne, the result of an autoimmune disorder similar to lupus.

To break the ice during interviews, I chatted informally with the women before I began the audio recording of our conversation. As we talked, Christina remarked that because she had grown up in poverty, she craved financial stability. In search of that, she had scratched her way to the middle class by opening the home daycare business, which later allowed her to purchase several apartment buildings that generated additional income.

Like most Americans, Christina described herself as "a middle-class person who works every day, trying to make ends meet, trying to have a successful life for me and my children." As our interview shifted to healthcare, Christina described the challenges of striving for upward mobility as a Black woman:

> Yeah, I've always felt it's a burden being Black, health-wise, education-wise, getting benefits for certain things, you know, 'cause sometimes when you apply for it you're just another Black person trying to get something for free or another Black person trying to get some handout.

Christina's reflection implies a fight for legitimacy, to be viewed as a rights-bearing citizen deserving of healthcare, education, or other services. She touches on the intractable stereotypes of Black women, such as "welfare queens" who are always on the take, and suggests that the work she does to differentiate herself from these labels is difficult.

Later, she described that, although her hold on middle-class life was sometimes shaky, Christina was proud that her entrepreneurialism augmented her family's income. She was also relieved that, unlike in her childhood, in which she was relegated to seeking care from doctors who accepted "medical cards,"[1] she had employer-sponsored health insurance through her husband. In spite of this security, she described multiple instances in which she felt she was stereotyped as the Mammy image[2] most commonly associated with Aunt Jemima advertisements:

> Before, I had a doctor, I thought she was very racist. That's why I let her go. She would really say stuff, like, "You're fat." But when I was in the waiting room one day, the lady told me, "I had her before, and I had to let her go. Yeah, because she don't like Black people. She don't like fat people." This lady was Black, and she was overweight, too. I was like, "I had a problem with her before, and I thought it was just me." She said, "Na-uh.'"

Christina interpreted her provider's disdain for fat[3] women as a form of racial discrimination and went so far as to discuss it with another patient in the waiting area.

Although we cannot know the provider's opinions of her patients, Christina believed that she held negative stereotypes about Black women, particularly Black women of non-normative body size. Eventually, Christina changed providers even though she thought she was a "good doctor." Christina's experience with her doctor is telling in that, regardless of the doctor's motivation, Christina did not trust her to provide unbiased, fair, and empathetic care. Christina left a "good" physician because she felt that ultimately her doctor's biases would lead to lower quality treatment.

Christina's experience illustrates the intersection of an age-old stereotype of Black women (i.e., the Mammy) and contemporary framing of the "obesity epidemic." Obesity is described as an intractable public health crisis that disproportionately affects Black women. According to the Centers for Disease Control and Prevention more than half (56.9%) of Black adult women are obese

---

[1] Medical cards refer to the public health insurance, or Medicaid, programs for the poor. Because many physicians do not accept Medicaid due to low reimbursement rates, low-income people are limited in their choice of provider.

[2] See Chapter 1 for a full discussion of stereotypes of Black women including the Sapphire, Mammy, and Jezebel. The Mammy stereotype is in contrast to the sexually available Jezebel. Mammy had no sexual desires, was docile and maternal, and, perhaps most importantly, was fat, dark-skinned, and unfeminine (Harris-Perry, 2011).

[3] In some activist, feminist, and queer communities, the term "fat" is the preferred descriptor as opposed to "overweight," which assumes there is a known, "healthy" normative weight. Fat activists prefer the term "fat" because they feel it reclaims the neutral description of the body without the normative value judgment associated with the term "overweight" (Rothblum & Solovay, 2009).

(as measured by their body mass index [BMI]) compared to 35.5% of White women, 45.7% of Latina women, and 11.9% of Asian women (Ogden, Carroll, Fryar, & Flegal, 2015). Given the overwhelmingly negative messaging around obesity, Black women may be hypervigilant to the potential negative health consequences of their weight and simultaneously resistant to the particular disdain for Black, fat women. In Christina's case, although she acknowledged wanting to lose weight, she was frustrated by her provider's contempt for her size, which she interpreted as a form of racial discrimination. Given the pervasive negative stereotypes of fat people, coupled with the Mammy stereotype of Black women in particular, Christina's assessment seems quite plausible.

However, perhaps the most important point of Christina's story is that it suggests that her perception of being stereotyped and discriminated against caused her to forego treatment and seek another doctor. In this manner, Christina's story may explain how the perception of bias and discrimination delays treatment and ultimately leads to poorer health outcomes.

Leona and Christina both described experiences in which they had to manage doctors' perceptions of them while simultaneously paying attention to the information provided by the physician. Based on these data, I argue that the nature of the patient–provider relationship for Black middle-class women is likely quite different from that of the majority middle class. While many people walk into the doctor's office with a sense of unease or trepidation about their health problem or irritation over being rushed through appointments, the women in this study suggested that, in addition to these universal concerns, they faced the extra hurdle of wondering if their doctor treats them differently because they are Black women. They were vigilant to cues about how the provider evaluated them, which led to uncertainty and more questions: for example, does the provider treat me this way because I'm a Black woman (a fat woman; a disabled, fat, Black woman)? How do I know if I am being treated fairly? How do I evaluate what is happening in the exam room? How do I get the best care for myself? And, Can I still receive "high-quality" medical care from a provider who holds biased or stereotyped views? Given this backdrop, it is very difficult for Black women to evaluate whether their provider has the necessary combination of quality medical knowledge, sound science, and good social skills.

Leona and Christina, like other women in the study, described trying to adjust to persistent stereotyping in many settings, including healthcare, public spaces, and employment. However, in contrast to the social science and popular narratives of Black victimization, the women I interviewed also emphasized the strategies they used to resist stereotyping in the doctors' office, a space that is supposedly safe. Although Black middle-class women may be able to quickly and cogently describe their health concerns, understand and use medical terminology, and follow the particular logic of Western biomedical discourse, the need to enact these strategies under such high stakes must be exhausting and disempowering. Leona, Christina, and the other women with whom I spoke described a feeling of being caught between a rock and hard place with their provider when the main goal was to put their health first. The remainder of this chapter takes up the specific strategies women use to manage the healthcare encounter.

"Dressing the Part": Physical Presentation in Healthcare Settings

> I have went to the doctor's office in jeans. Sometimes I went dressy.... one day I wore my Coach purse, and my shoes, and they said, "You look so good. Where did you get that purse from?" ... I do think they look at you different, like, "You've got that diamond ring on your finger? She might report me if I don't treat her right." But you walking around with some raggedy shoes, and your hair sticking out, I think they might say, "She ain't going to report me."
> —Christina describing how she dresses for doctor's visits

During the interviews and focus groups, I asked women about their strategies to deal with doctors, including whether they took particular care with their clothing and other grooming.[4] Their responses highlight the fact that, for women's bodies in general and particularly for the Black female body, the way people perceive them is complicated by racial, sexual, and class stereotypes. The women were uniformly concerned about how they presented themselves in public settings, and healthcare was no exception. Christina's comment illustrated some of the main themes echoed by the majority of the women. For Christina, clothing and accessories communicated social privilege and cues of favorable economic and social status.

Interestingly, Christina felt that wearing certain clothing or accessories gave the impression she was a person to be taken seriously and suggested that if healthcare providers think you are well off financially they are more likely to treat you well. Christina also alluded to the fact that her concerns were taken more seriously if people believed she had money, or at least they believed she was "not poor," a central concern for a group of people who are often lumped into the category of the "Black poor." For Christina and many other women, the dominant narrative of Black poverty and, by extension, Black pathology,

[4] These data are not meant to suggest Black women should have to wear certain clothing to go to the doctor or enact any strategies to try to get the best care. They are presented to better understand the barriers women of color face in healthcare settings and do not imply that women should have to dress or behave in a way to be treated fairly.

followed them into the healthcare encounter, which led them to exert substantial effort to play against type.

Another respondent, Lee, alluded to a sense of pride in trying to look nice when she went to the doctor. Lee is a 57-year-old licensed practical nurse who was raised in Mississippi. She suffered from many chronic illnesses and also recently survived an acute life-threatening infection. She stated:

> I always try to look nice when I go to the doctor. Even if I'm feeling bad,
> I try to look real nice and neat. . . . And I don't care how bad I feel, you
> can never tell it by looking at me.

Lee exerted a significant amount of effort to look presentable. Even in a weakened or vulnerable condition, she still felt the need to present herself as though she were not sick. Similar to Christina, Lee hinted at the importance of impression management even in the context of the significant physical and emotional vulnerability people often experience in the face of illness.

Other women reported similar attitudes. For example, a focus group participant implied that because of Black women's vulnerable position in society, presentation was extremely important.

> And look it, as African Americans, we were told—I was told—never
> to go to the doctor looking worn down and torn down, to always come
> together. But you think if I took the time to get myself together, I wasn't
> as sick? No. My mother told me to always have something together.
> —Focus group participant in her 50s

This woman implied that because Black women are often devalued in American society, pride in one's personal appearance is essential to maintaining a sense of self and projecting competency to the broader world, both in general and in healthcare settings. The women in the study seemed to anticipate being devalued based on their race and gender and tried to manage their self-presentation to soften the blow. Taken together, the women's comments highlight the importance of communicating social privilege and material resources through manner of dress. Furthermore, they point to a Black cultural construct that emphasizes personal grooming and suggests taking care with one's dress reflects racial pride and mitigates the assumption that all Blacks are poor (Leeds Craig, 2002).

Another woman, Vanessa, suggested that race and gender stereotypes were powerful forces in Black women's lives. When asked about the importance of physical presentation in healthcare, Vanessa stated:

Oh, I think that's important. If you come into whatever that person's perception is of a lower-class person or whatever, I don't think you're going to be treated that well.

So before you open your mouth or anything, image is everything. You come in there with some shorts up to your behind, and they're gonna think that you're some kind of hoochie or something, well, then you're gonna be treated that way. So if you want respect, you need to dress the part.

Vanessa hinted at the tension between trying to avoid living up to common stereotypes of Black people (i.e., that they are all poor) and the particular stereotype of Black women (i.e., "the hoochie" or Jezebel). Curiously, Vanessa felt that it was *her* responsibility, not the provider's, to behave in a way that garnered respect, suggesting that she internalized the respectability politics that have infused much of the discourse on the Black experience. Vanessa also seemed to distance herself from poorer race-mates in what sociologist Karyn Lacy terms *boundary work*, the effort middle-class Blacks make to differentiate themselves from poorer Blacks (Lacy, 2007).

"Demonstrate That You Are Also a Person": Women's Efforts to Connect with Doctors

I think that they first look at me as being inferior because of my gender. I think they look at me being even more inferior because of my race and therefore I think a lot of people get surprised when they realize that you are intelligent, you are articulate, you work hard to communicate accurately . . . I think they also get surprised when you demonstrate that you are also a person.

I think that makes a difference, too. You've got to click in order for them to understand that, hey, I'm not chopped liver here. But I think that, unfortunately, the onus is on the patient to be aggressive, oh, that's terrible, isn't it?

—Chris, 59, doctorate in divinity

Although many women agreed that the way they dressed was important, the majority of them tried to connect with the doctor with the specific purpose of resisting stereotypes of Black women. Like Chris, many women in the study felt the need to differentiate themselves from common tropes about Black women.

For Chris, a short, zaftig woman with a round face, cropped tight curls, and cocoa butter skin, a doctorate in divinity and a high-powered career at a university did not protect against the illegitimacy of being Black and female. Chris was quick-witted, and her comments about healthcare providers suggested she was determined to be recognized as a human being apart from the prevailing stereotypes that surrounded her. She seemed acutely aware of the particular gender and race stereotypes that may have led providers to devalue her intelligence. Chris also described her use of specific elements of cultural health capital, like conveying health-related information in a medically intelligible and efficient manner. As she described her experiences with doctors, she emphasized the effort it took to conform to the unwritten and unacknowledged expectations of some healthcare providers. However, the energy she expended to meet these expectations is invisible.

Furthermore, because Chris was middle-class and highly educated, she used her cultural acumen and verbal skills to connect with the provider, presumably to secure better interpersonal treatment than would be possible in the absence of these skills. However, her statement that the onus is on the patient to be aggressive suggests that this type of adjustment is burdensome. Political scientist and pundit Melissa Harris-Perry (2011) contends that Black women are "misrecognized" or denied their common humanity and citizenship in the American polity and psyche, which leads them to work hard to hold on to their individuality. Chris's analysis of the ways in which race, class, and gender affect her suggest she is "misrecognized" or rendered invisible in healthcare settings as well.

Although Chris clearly stated that she tried to connect with the provider, she also lamented that while she did what she could to minimize stereotyping and discrimination, there are many situations in which no amount of articulation, nice clothing, or other markers of class status make any difference. For example, she described a situation in which her doctor referred her to a health club to begin an exercise regimen. She stated,

> I think that how you present yourself, your education . . . your educational persona is going to affect how you are going to be received and treated. But then last week at the health club, my husband and I walked in. My husband is a retired professor and I am Jamaican. And the people at the desk wanted to know what we were doing there, and did we have an appointment, and they even called up to the rehab center to make sure that we were legitimate. So even educational level and how you present yourself sometimes doesn't make a darn bit of difference.

Again, Chris suggested that Black people continue to face daily discrimination regardless of their ability to emphasize educational attainment or "discipline" their bodies through exercise. She conveyed a sense of frustration and indicated that, in spite of her educational "persona," she is delegitimized even when attempting to conform to American society's emphasis on personal responsibility through exercise. Taking an instrumental approach to one's body is also a key component of cultural health capital (Shim, 2010). In this instance, Chris's education, career, or commitment to exercise cannot mitigate prevailing notions of Black illegitimacy.

Her comments also imply that she exerted a substantial effort to be recognized as an individual separate from generalizations of Black women. Chris indicated that, in spite of her status as an educated professional person, she was not always able to override the negative stereotypes of Black people. This is in keeping with Harris-Perry's and other scholarship on the intrapsychic lives of Black women, which theorizes that because stereotypes of Black people are so pervasive, and so overwhelmingly negative, Black women feel an intense pressure to counter the stereotypes and, by extension, be recognized as individuals (Jones & Shorter-Gooden, 2003).

Chris also touched on a fundamental human desire to construct a personhood and to be recognized as a human being. These existential concerns are certainly universal, although I argue that, because of the context of the Black experience in the United States, this effort takes on a particular meaning for Black women who have always struggled to be viewed as rights-bearing citizens. Women in this study echoed the unique existential concerns of Black women by resisting negative characterizations and pushing against a constrained range of options for Black women. Certainly women of all races and ethnic backgrounds struggle against sexism and other forms of oppression. However, the women in this study imply that their attempts to connect with their healthcare provider come with the extra effort to be seen as a person apart from the pervasive stereotypes of Black women.

With few exceptions, the women in the study strongly identified with the need to forge a personal connection with their healthcare provider. Furthermore, their experiences and perceptions of healthcare providers were similar regardless of their education or class status. Overall, the women described what I would argue is the universal experience of seeking recognition as an individual—mediated by the unique position Black women occupy in American society. That is to say, because the healthcare experience is often intimate and vulnerable, everyone would like to be treated with individual attention and respect. For Black women, this may be an even bigger struggle given the historical and contemporary context of the Black American experience.

Armed with Information: Knowledge as a Weapon
in the Fight for Legitimacy

> I come in so armed with information that you can look at me and want
> to put me in this box but the minute I start talking about some words
> that you know you read in a book somewhere it's completely different!
> —Tracey, 35, self-employed

Tracey, a single woman with an MBA, arrived at the focus group[5] with a buoyant attitude and big curly hair to match. She had recently left a stable job to start her own consulting business, a decision that required all her bravery and confidence. Tall in stature and sturdily built, Tracey had a lot to say about how she dealt with doctors.

Like Christina and other women in the study, Tracey's physicality seemed to play an outsize role in her healthcare experiences. During the focus group she explained why she felt the need to come in "armed with information" designed to counteract the stereotypes, or "box," she faced as a Black woman. Tracey used the image of being "armed with information" almost as a shield or tool to resist the dominant perceptions of Black women. And, as she explained her story to the other women in the focus group, it became abundantly clear why she used such a strong metaphor.

As an undergraduate student, Tracy began suffering from pain in her right knee. Eventually, the pain began to interfere with her daily activities and she sought help from many physicians who ordered x-rays that turned up nothing. Tracey explained:

> In undergraduate, I woke up one day and my knee was bothering me and I went to a doctor and they said nothing was wrong. And I went to another doctor and they did an x-ray and they said nothing was wrong.... I would go for a year
> and I would go back to somebody else and they would tell me nothing was wrong. And then 15 years elapsed ...
> [Eventually] I went to a doctor and I said, look, it hurts so bad at night ... the only way I can sleep through the night is to take Advil before going to bed. And he said well you just have to do that for the rest of your life.

[5] This section refers to data collected from one of two focus groups I conducted to better understand variation between the healthcare experiences of lower middle-class compared to upper middle-class Black women. A full description of the methods used for this study appears in the methods appendix.

Half the time they were telling me it was because of [my] weight, they put me in physical therapy, they did all these things. And I was young and I still believed in the myth that doctors were infallible.

Although Tracey delivered her story dispassionately, it is important to note how long she dealt with the pain, how young she was when it first began, and how many healthcare providers dismissed her concerns. She became so disillusioned that, eventually, after years of suffering, she gave up on ever getting answers or relief from the pain. In fact, Tracey's experience exemplifies what we know about racial differences in pain management. In the United States, Black people are systematically undertreated for pain compared to White people (Hoffman, Trawalter, Axt, & Oliver, 2016). For example, a 2016 study published in the *Proceedings of the National Academy of Sciences* found that a substantial number of White lay people, medical students, and residents hold the erroneous belief that Blacks are biologically different (i.e., better able to withstand pain) from Whites. The study's authors found that these erroneous beliefs predicted the provider's assessment of patient discomfort and the accuracy of the provider's subsequent treatment recommendation (Hoffman et al., 2016). Tracey's experience, in which she was told to simply deal with the pain, is an example of how these differences in treatment affect people every day and for years at a time. However, because multiple providers ignored her pleas for help, Tracey's suffering was also rendered invisible.

In spite of Tracey's decision to avoid healthcare providers all together, after a minor car accident required her to get a check-up, she found a physician who had come highly recommended by a friend. Thankfully, this physician seemed to take her concerns seriously and ordered a magnetic resonance imaging (MRI) study of her knee. The scan yielded troubling results, and she was told to come back to the hospital immediately:

They called me and said you need to come back . . . they set me up for surgery and I had two tumors in my knee that had been growing for 15 years that nobody found . . . . [After the surgery] I was out of work 2 months; I was in physical therapy for 9 months because of what they did and as the doctor explained to me had they [the tumors] been malignant . . . they would have had to amputate.

Tracey's story is deeply troubling. Over the course of 15 years, only one physician took the time to order a more sensitive diagnostic imaging test like an MRI (as opposed to an x-ray), which ultimately led to the proper diagnosis and treatment. In spite of her status as a middle-class, educated woman pursuing her undergraduate degree and later an MBA, Tracey was never viewed as a credible witness to her own condition. The question, of course, is why do Black women have such a hard time being viewed as legitimate healthcare citizens?

When I asked Tracey how she viewed her experience and whether she thought race or gender affected how she was treated, she noted that, like Christina, weight seemed to play a big role in her care.

> I think if anything it was the weight; that becomes something that is an easy answer. Rather than race, I think it was a set of solutions.

Tracey felt that physicians used her weight as a shorthand to explain all her health problems. She explained that when presented with a healthcare puzzle, weight became the de facto solution. Tracey used a math analogy to explain:

> What's 2 plus 2? It's 5. What's 3 plus 6? It's 5.
> It's only one answer because of the weight. I think sometimes it's a set of solutions that I [in referring to the doctor] let myself consider when I treat you.

Unlike Christina, Tracey interpreted her negative experiences as being solely about her weight and not necessarily about contempt for fat people in general or fat Black women in particular. Tracey felt strongly that her weight impeded the judgment of multiple providers who were unable to critically evaluate her presenting complaint.

Although Tracey did not view her experience as being related to race and gender, other women in the focus group noted that, just because Tracey did not think it was race or gender discrimination, it still could have been. It is impossible to suss out the viewpoint of multiple providers or tease out the independent effect of race, class, gender, weight, and the like. Regardless, focusing on parsing the individual effect of race, class, gender, or weight discrimination misses the point. People arrive at the doctor as a whole person who may be female, fat, Black, tall, or whatever, and they deal with the consequences of the doctor's perception of them overall.

For Tracey, and many others in the study, these experiences redoubled her commitment to fiercely advocate for herself by conducting research prior to the healthcare encounter. In a 2013 study of physicians, medical sociologist Leslie Dubbin and colleagues found conveying medical information in a succinct and rational manner and demonstrating intelligence were critical to being viewed as legitimate, credible patients (Dubbin, Chang, & Shim, 2013). The majority of women I interviewed strongly expressed the belief that conducting research was almost a prerequisite for a successful visit. For example, Vanessa stated:

Oh, I think it's important, right up front, so they know then they don't have to waste time trying to tell you, give you instructions on what to do. That is gonna set them up, too, to treat you in a certain way, because they know that you're a little more knowledgeable.

—Vanessa, 50, divorced, owner of image consulting business

Vanessa's comments illustrate a certain form of currency that seems increasingly important in healthcare settings: the ability to communicate in an intelligible and efficient manner. Vanessa hinted at the need to convey medically relevant information quickly and succinctly to convey her own intelligence. Although the contemporary healthcare context universally emphasizes medical consumerism, these pressures may disproportionately affect Black women.

Another respondent, Patty, echoed this sentiment:

I think it helps when you let them know that you did look it up online. Yeah. Their eyes open like oh. Okay. I got to be on this. And maybe they see that you are trying to take part in your healing, too.

—Patty, 52, writer

Patty seemed to suggest that she bears the responsibility to signal her motivation, which, in turn, cues the provider that they must take her more seriously as a patient.

Taken together, the women's comments illustrate the perceived importance of conveying legitimacy, motivation, and mastery of biomedical terminology.

Although women felt strongly about the need to do research on their health condition prior to the encounter, they also noted a potential downside. Several women said they had to be careful not to insult the physician or challenge his or her position. For example, Fran, a 46-year-old mother of four who owns an academic tutoring business, stated:

It's a delicate balance—you don't want to make it seem like you know more than the doctor. But you want to let the doctor know that you're informed. And that you know how to research these things. And maybe they'll be more rigorous then. . . . You want to have some respect for it [the medical profession], but you want to make sure that they're doing their job.

Fran's reticence to challenge the physician is in keeping with psychologist Burgess and colleagues (2006) who found that physicians may interpret a White patient asking questions as a legitimate attempt to collect information and demonstrate their mastery of medical terminology, whereas minority patients may be viewed as questioning the provider's expertise and authority.

Another study participant, Marie, a 47-year-old divorced mother and police detective, noted that she was careful not to overemphasize the research she conducted for fear of damaging her relationship with the provider. She stated:

> If they said something to me, I would say okay, I need to look into that to myself. I wouldn't let them know all that I knew. I didn't think that was helpful to me in my relationship with them.

Fran and Marie imply that, because the physician is the person in a power position, any attempt to display specific healthcare knowledge may also be interpreted as a challenge to the physician's authority.

Bella's story further illustrates the complexity of self-advocacy with healthcare providers. Bella, a 55-year-old divorced mother of two who runs a nonprofit organization, had recently sought the care of a podiatrist for bunion surgery. Although bunion surgery typically involves shaving down the bones of the foot, Bella was displeased that the surgeon removed a bone in her foot without explicitly explaining the procedure. However, she was reluctant to complain or ask follow-up questions. She explained:

> I come to find out when I went back for a check-up they had removed a bone from my foot . . . and they put a screw in my foot. I'm like, "Since when do you get rid of bunions and calluses and get bone removed and screws?"
>
> They didn't explain that. I thought I didn't have to ask that. . . . And so I blame myself to this day.
>
> Let me tell you something: as a Black woman, life is hard as it is. And when you're by yourself, you're out there struggling, trying to do things. So my thoughts were not to get rebellious; I didn't even think about it, to get rebellious. I was like, "Damn," 'cause I didn't even know it for a while, until I went to have x- rays done, and that's when I found out. And I was like, "Damn, I should've done something."

Bella was clearly distrustful of medical institutions and providers. But her comments also suggest that the accumulation of moving through the world as a Black woman had also left her battle-scarred. Like many other Black Americans of a certain age, Bella had grown up in Mississippi during the Jim Crow era in which Black people were subjected to separate and sub-par public accommodations, including healthcare (Washington, 2006). As such, her mistrust and reluctance to question her provider is hardly surprising. Given that medical exploitation (e.g., the Tuskegee Syphilis Experiment, forced sterilizations of Black women, and sub-par medical treatment) was overwhelmingly the norm in the South, Bella's apprehension is more than understandable (Gamble, 1993; Roberts, 1997; Washington, 2006).

However, in addition to the daily indignities Black people endured in the Jim Crow south, Bella survived sexual exploitation at the hands of her physician. Bella was extremely reticent to question the doctor, which may be explained by her experience enduring segregated healthcare facilities (and other accommodations) in the South:

> I was 16, and it was in Mississippi. There were two doctors who worked in that *facility* . . . they had the Colored side and the White side. I used to fuss every time my mom took me in. "Why we gotta sit on this side with the old furniture? I wanna sit over there," you know? [Her mom would say] "Shut up, shut up." That's what she used to tell me. "Just be quiet; it's okay, just be quiet." I'm like, "No, it's not."

Later, Bella referred to a doctor who sexually molested her during a medical exam:

> Dr. Turner—he could drink a lot, too. And when he was examining me, he used to feel my breasts, and then when he'd examine me down there, he'd do little things.
> And he [Dr. Turner] did something down there—I don't know what he did—but ever since then, I got this little—it's this little tingle that I can feel down there when I'm having sex.

Undoubtedly, it is important to recognize Bella's childhood experience of enduring the indignities of segregation, sub-par medical facilities, and sexual molestation by a White physician to better understand her contemporary healthcare experience. As a child under the extreme racial regime of Jim Crow, Bella learned that she was powerless to question the socially sanctioned authority that promoted "separate but unequal" facilities. She was also unable to advocate for herself as an adolescent Black girl being sexually molested by a White physician. Even years later, at the time of the interview, Bella was unsure what the doctor had done to such an intimate part of her body. Yet she was forced to live with the uncertainty of not knowing what really happened and the constant physical reminder of the physician's predation and exploitation.

Bella described a childhood in which racial domination was omnipresent and omnipotent. As an adult, Bella recounted her struggle as a Black woman and lamented that she was not in a position to get "rebellious." Presumably, she equated rebelliousness with the capacity to advocate on her own behalf. Bella's story reminds us that, regardless of an individual's current SES, or ability to self-discipline through exercise, research, or manner of dress, our past experiences indelibly shape the present. For many Black people in the United States, particularly those who grew up in the South and later came to Northern cities during the Great Migration, the racial and sexual trauma do not simply disappear.

Although Bella was certainly entitled to ask questions of her provider, she did not and ultimately regretted her reticence to do so. But who could blame her? The horrible abuse and trauma she suffered as a child must certainly affect Bella's engagement with healthcare providers in the present. How could she be expected to "get rebellious" or advocate for herself given the context in which she grew up? Bella's account of the healthcare experiences throughout her life hint at the strong poles Black women are often torn between. They must be careful not to come across as too powerful or masculine while always living up to the trope of the "strong Black woman" who can "make a way out of no way."

Bella's experience illustrates a double-bind to which many Black women can relate.

Although the women reported that it is important to conduct research and demonstrate their ability to comprehend medical information, Black women walk a fine line between self-advocacy and challenging the doctor's role. While Dubbin et al. (2013) note that providers have specific expectations of what makes a capable and proficient patient, at least some have an overarching expectation of compliance with medical recommendations. A physician respondent in the Dubbin's et al. study remarked, "They have to believe I know what I'm talking about. They can argue, but they do have to comply" (p. 116). The provider holds considerable power over his or her patients and ultimately controls the assessment of the patient's condition and subsequent treatment recommendations. However, these findings suggest that Black middle-class women are aware that they must advocate for themselves while avoiding overt challenges to the provider. The women in this study also suggest that the specific biases Black women face are particularly confining in a context in which the provider possesses an unnamed set of expectations that intersect with race and gender stereotypes.

Legitimacy, History, and the Healthcare Encounter

Although the majority of American health disparities research focuses on poor African Americans, these data highlight the ongoing significance of race and gender for Black women who are not poor. Leona, Christina, Tracey, Chris, Bella and others enacted their own strategies to be viewed as a legitimate individuals worthy of quality healthcare.

Unfortunately, their experiences indicate that structural discrimination negatively affects Black women's health across the board.

Furthermore, although the results of social science studies are always open for interpretation, I argue that the findings presented here should reorient us to the cumulative and historical nature of contemporary social problems. Although social scientists typically study the causes of health and social problems in the contemporary moment, apart from the historical context, these data demonstrate how the past insinuates itself into the present.

The study also suggests that almost no form of self-advocacy or healthcare consumerism can override the perception of illegitimacy Black middle-class women face in healthcare settings. The women's stories highlight the need for more nuanced training and education in medical schools to better understand that, given the particular historical and contemporary context for Black people, class does not shield one from discrimination in healthcare settings.[6] History follows us into the exam room, both in the form of the historical arrangements that led to race and gender discrimination and in the ways Black women anticipate discrimination when interacting with predominantly White institutions. These experiences must be acknowledged as straining and potentially burdensome.

Ultimately, this may explain why Black women at every level of SES have worse outcomes than similar White women (Jackson & Cummings, 2011). The strain of this performance certainly accumulates over time. And one must wonder what, in turn, is also lost as discrimination insinuates itself into annual physicals, second opinions, and everything that goes along with keeping oneself healthy. As much as women in this study used very specific strategies to try to mitigate stereotypes and bias, there is often very little that can be done to avoid unconscious (or conscious) bias.

Last, the women I interviewed reflected on the social inequities (i.e., race and gender stereotyping) that led them to believe they should perform in a certain way. As such, their stories implicate a larger system of inequality and must not be interpreted to suggest people should have to behave in a certain way to receive adequate medical care. I am not arguing that wearing certain clothing, emphasizing medical terminology, or other makers of class status should be thought of as interventions to reduce health disparities. Rather, the women's experiences should serve as a critique of the social arrangements that give rise to such disparities and the strategies women use to mitigate them.

In addition, although the study participants were more socioeconomically privileged than many African Americans, their stories implicate the ongoing

[6] I am not suggesting that poor people do not deserve unbiased, high-quality healthcare. Instead, I am focusing our attention on inequalities that remain among the middle and upper classes so that we can better understand how race and gender discrimination affects healthcare across all groups.

significance of race, class, and gender in shaping healthcare. For the women in this study, pulling out all the stops to do research, engage the provider, or wear nice clothes was a way of standing up for themselves in the context of the patient–provider relationship, in which the patient has substantially less power than the provider. For racial and gender minorities, the power difference may be that much more acute. As a result, Black women, regardless of their class status, feel the need to perform, jockey, or otherwise fight for recognition. At least, as Black middle-class women, they have more resources to bring to bear on the encounter. However, as these data demonstrate, these resources do not necessarily mitigate discrimination. The fact that Black, American, middle-class women, with their relative privileges, continue to face these challenges certainly does not bode well for other groups with multiple disadvantages, including the poor and disabled, patients who do not communicate well in English, undocumented patients, and so forth. In this manner, these stories serve as a litmus test for the healthcare system's ability to successfully treat society's most vulnerable.

Finally, we must consider the emotional and physiological toll of these day-to-day performances. Malat et al. (Malat, van Ryn, & Purcell, 2006), Geronimus (1996), Krieger and Sidney (1996), Clark et al. (Clark, Anderson, Clark, & Williams, 1999), and many other scholars have described this type of exertion as an additional stressor or burden that has been linked to poor health among Black people in the United States. These stressors likely exert a cumulative physiological effect (McEwen & Seeman, 1999) that may explain why African Americans have worse health outcomes at every level of income and education compared to similar White people. When it comes to healthcare, the stakes are very high. However, the stakes for women in this study, including Tracey, who suffered significant pain and could have lost her leg, and Christina, who left the care of a competent provider because she was concerned about receiving fair treatment, could not be higher. Bias, stereotyping, and discrimination may literally cost you your life.

3

Patient Preferences

The Relative (Un)Importance of Race and Gender
Concordance

Old sins cast long shadows.
—Danish proverb

And I wouldn't care if you were purple with pink polka dots. If you can
do what I need or I want, I don't give a, as I call it, a flying flip on a rolling donut, as long as you and I can get me where I need to go.
—Ellen, 60, IT sales

Ellen, an ebullient woman with short grayish hair and a penchant for gourmet
cooking, was one of the first women I interviewed for this study. Although much
of the research literature emphasizes pairing Black patients with Black providers to reduce healthcare disparities, Ellen seemed particularly nonplussed when
I asked her if she preferred a Black doctor. She had recently survived a brain
aneurysm under the care of doctors of all racial backgrounds, so the idea that
she would prefer a Black doctor seemed to strike her as absurd. But, given that
the research literature has generally upheld "race concordance" as an effective
strategy for reducing differences in treatment, I wanted to learn more about
how women evaluated race and gender concordance and if it affected women's
experiences at the doctor overall (Blanchard, Nayar, & Lurie, 2007; LaVeist,
Nuru-Jeter, & Jones, 2003; Schinkel, Schouten, Street, van den Putte, & van
Weert, 2016).

A large body of research literature on healthcare disparities suggests that
increasing the proportion of healthcare visits in which Black doctors treat Black
patients may reduce differences in treatment. This strategy, termed "race concordance," makes sense on its face particularly given that up to 75% African
Americans receive healthcare in racially discordant patient–provider pairs
(Chen, Fryer, Phillips, Wilson, & Pathman, 2005). That is to say, almost three-
quarters of African Americans are treated by a non–African American provider.
As I argued in a previous chapter, healthcare may be accurately characterized as
a predominately White institution, a "White space" where Black patients must
do what they can to mitigate how they are judged and appraised. However, as

psychiatrist Jonathan Metzl (2010) cautions, the structural inequities that likely produce health disparities occur long before the patient enters the exam room. Furthermore, the pervasive stereotypes of Black women I outlined in the previous chapter affect how Black people think about and appraise other Black people. Therefore, simply placing a Black patient with a Black provider is unlikely to alter the fundamental causes of healthcare inequities. That said, given the durability of differences in treatment, one would be hard pressed to argue against increasing the proportion of race- (and gender-) concordant treatment encounters.

However, the race concordance hypothesis rests on the largely untested assumption that minority patients prefer to be treated by providers of the same race or ethnic group and that receiving treatment from a minority provider leads to better communication, less interpersonal discomfort, and better health outcomes (Cooper et al., 2003; LaVeist et al., 2003). However, the empirical research has produced mixed results about whether minorities even prefer a same-race provider and the extent to which concordance increases their satisfaction with the healthcare encounter (Chen et al., 2005; LaVeist & Nuru-Jeter, 2002; LaVeist et al., 2003). For example, using a nationally representative sample, health services researchers Malat and van Ryn (2005) found that only 20% of African Americans preferred a provider of the same race. Regardless of whether minority patients prefer a minority provider, the empirical evidence is inconclusive as to whether race concordance actually improves patient health outcomes, patient– provider communication, and perceptions of respect (Meghani et al., 2009; Sacks, 2013; Shen et al., 2017; Sweeney, Zinner, Rust, & Fryer, 2016).

In keeping with previous studies, the findings of my work also paint a complex and sometimes contradictory picture of race and gender preferences among middle-class Black women.[1] This chapter comprises five sections that explore the complexity of these so-called preferences. First, I present a case study of Tammy, a focus group respondent whose great-grandfather was involved in an infamous medical study conducted by the US government.[2] In many ways, Tammy's case illustrates and supports the underlying assumptions of the race concordance hypothesis; that is, that (a) Black patients want Black providers; (b) having a Black provider guards against discriminatory or unequal treatment; and (c) in the absence of discrimination, Black patients will receive the same treatment as their White counterparts.

---

[1] This study is based on in-depth interviews and focus groups with Black women who were lower middle to upper middle class. A full description of the research methods, including who was in the study sample, how I recruited participants, and how I analyzed the data appears in the methods appendix.

[2] A description of the study follows in the next section.

However, her story also points to the *longue duree* of structural discrimination, in healthcare settings and in general, thus reminding us that the causes of healthcare inequities precede the two people in the exam room.

Second, I contrast Tammy's case with the remainder of study respondents who complicated the underlying assumptions of the race concordance hypothesis by emphasizing (a) the intersection of race, gender, and other identities (e.g., disability, age, sexual orientation etc.) on the formulation of preferences; (b) the futility of race concordance as a strategy to mitigate the effects of a rushed, impersonal, and neo-liberal healthcare environment; (c) intraracial tensions that may lead some Black women to avoid Black providers, thereby turning the race concordance assumption on its head; and (d) using the race of the provider as a proxy for the overall quality of the healthcare facility itself. These tensions may arise in the face of society's stubborn anti-Blackness, which necessarily leads to sub-par healthcare facilities in predominantly Black communities.

Part 1

The Past as Present: Tammy's Story

As I interviewed women for this study, I was frequently intrigued, and sometimes befuddled, by what they had to say about their encounters with healthcare providers. Their comments often confirmed existing research about differences in treatment, but many times they diverged from the current state of the field. Given that an implicit purpose of qualitative research is to discover new concepts or knowledge that would be difficult to glean using quantitative methods, I was curious when a discussion emerged during one of the focus groups I conducted with upper middle-class[3] Black women.

I began the focus group by encouraging study participants to speak freely and without regard to how their comments would be received by the other respondents. I also asked that they keep the conversation confidential so that people would feel free to speak their mind. I asked them what kind of doctor they preferred; that is, did they want a female or male provider; Black, White, or non-White providers. Based on my read of the research literature, I expected their

---

[3] The purpose of this study was to analyze the healthcare experiences of non-poor Black women. As such, I recruited women who would be considered lower middle class (e.g., having some college education or less) compared to upper middle-class women (having a college degree and middle household income). Research on health outcomes indicates that education is among the most significant predictors of health status so, based on these data, I used education as the criteria for inclusion in the study. For a more detailed description of the study's methods, see the research methods appendix.

answers to be simple enough to be conveyed by the term "preference" in a manner similar to the way people gravitate to certain styles of dress, food, or entertainment (e.g., "I prefer white wine over red"). However, as the group discussed their sometimes funny, awkward, or infuriating interactions with providers, the conversation took an unexpected turn when a young woman named Tammy shared her family's story. All of us were taken aback when Tammy said,

> My great-granddad was killed in the Tuskegee experiments, so my mother has a fit whenever I go—if I even seem like I may be seen by a non-Black doctor.

For Tammy, then a 37-year-old married mother of two who worked in finance, her family's involvement in the infamous Tuskegee Syphilis Study led to something much deeper than a simple preference for Black doctors.[4] Tammy was emphatic that not only would she prefer a Black physician, she would not allow anyone who was not Black to conduct any sort of medical intervention, however minor, on herself or her immediate family.

To fully appreciate the implications of Tammy's story, we must first understand the *Tuskegee Study of Syphilis in the Untreated Negro Male*.[5] The US Public Health Service (PHS) began the Study in 1932, and approximately 600 (399 syphilitics and 201 non-syphilitic controls) Black men from Macon County, Alabama, took part in it. They were never formally told they had syphilis. Instead, the PHS physicians leading the Study explained that they had "bad blood," which was a colloquialism that could refer to any number of conditions from anemia to diabetes (Jones, 1993). They also were led to believe that they would receive some kind of treatment for the condition. However, unknown to the men, the purpose of the Study was to determine whether the natural course of the disease progressed differently in Blacks than in Whites, which required

---

[4] Given Tammy's disclosure during the focus group, I wanted to have a more in-depth conversation with her to learn how the Tuskegee Syphilis Study had affected her family. Based on my research, there is very little scholarly analysis of the implications of the Study on the extended family members (Shakir, 2011). As such, I was fortunate that Tammy agreed to sit for an in-depth interview with me in 2015. The following section includes data from the focus group conducted in 2010 and the individual interview.

[5] "The Tuskegee Study of Untreated Syphilis in the Negro Male" is the original name of the Study. However, it has been referred to by many names including the US Public Health Service Study of Syphilis at Tuskegee and the Tuskegee Syphilis Experiment. Although the US Public Health Service conducted the Study, it is most closely associated with the Tuskegee Institute (now University). For the Tuskegee community, this name obscures the US government's responsibility for initiating, leading, and managing the Study for 40 years. For the purposes of this work, I will use the phrase "Tuskegee Syphilis Study" because that is how it is typically referred (Reverby, 2011).

withholding treatment. The idea was based in a commonly held notion of "racial dimorphism" in which the scientific and medical communities believed Blacks and Whites were fundamentally different biological entities, akin to different species[6] (Brandt, 1978; Hoberman, 2012). The effort to empirically validate *polygeny*, or the belief that different races were as biologically distinct as different species, began in the nineteenth century and sought to identify a ranking of races to demonstrate the intellectual superiority of Whites (Gould, 1996; Martin & Yeung, 2003). This research, much of which rested on dubious scientific practices even for their time, were used to support eugenic practices such as forced sterilization and rationalizations for the enslavement of Black people (Gould, 1996; Graves Jr. & Graves, 2003). Thus, the purpose of the Study was as pernicious in its aims as it was damaging to its involuntary participants. PHS never intended to provide treatment to the study respondents, and, although penicillin became available in 1943, the men were never treated with it. Many of the men also passed the infection to their wives, who subsequently went on to infect their children through congenital exposure (Washington, 2006).

The Study continued for 40 years and ended in 1972.

Although this troubling sequence of events seems relatively straightforward, the details of the Study and its implications remain contested. As historian and Tuskegee scholar Susan Reverby notes,

> The Tuskegee study is therefore an experience for which there is no longer a straightforward historical narrative, and moreover it cannot offer a simple morality tale. Rather, it exists in the liminal area of historical fog and fact, available as a set of experiences to be used by those who wish to tell differing tales, make various political points, and remember in discordant ways. As with other stories of critical importance in our national heritage, and especially those that focus on race and sexuality, the study endures on the cusp of memory and fact and in imagination, nightmare, and historical accounting at the same moment. (2001, pp. 22–23)

Reverby adeptly describes the Study as occupying the murky recesses of memory, which seemed particularly true for Tammy and her family in that, although the details of what happened to her great-grandfather were unclear, the effects of the Study were unequivocal. For many people who have experienced traumatic life events, the perception of reality is the only thing that matters. For example,

---

[6] Although racial dimorphism was a commonly held belief at the time, there is ample evidence that it persists in the present (Duster, 2005; Hatch, 2016; Hoberman, 2012; Kahn, 2013; Obasogie, Harris-Wai, Darling, Keagy, & Levesque, 2014; Reverby, 2008).

when I asked Tammy about her recollection of what happened to her great-grandfather she replied:

> And she [great-grandmother] had two kids with him [great-grandfather] and then he was in the Tuskegee experiment. And they sent him back and said that he had a spinal injury. . . . they sent him back in a box. And that's how he died . . . because they killed him and they kept it a secret. And that's the story that all of my elders will tell you now.

I asked Tammy about how the circumstances of her great-grandfather's death affected her view of medical professionals and she noted:

> That they were doing studies on him and that White doctors do studies on you. You can't trust White doctors because they'll give you medicine. It's not helping you. And you think it's fixing something. It's breaking three things.

When I asked Tammy how her family learned of the circumstances surrounding his death, her memory was less clear. She recounted a story in which her elder family members told her that her great-grandfather had left Lower Alabama (or LA as they called it) to seek better employment in the counties north of their home in southern Alabama. According to members of her church community, her great-grandfather returned to LA in a box. She recalled:

> It was for a job or some money. And they sent him back in a box . . . all the White folks said it was this and they said it was that. And it was lies. And some of the Black people were lying, too. And they wanted us to believe it and it was a lie because they killed him and kept it a secret.

The circumstances of her great-grandfather's death were obviously mysterious and cloaked in secrecy. She frequently repeated the idea that "they killed him and kept it a secret." Although I haven't been able to identify other instances of men being recruited from different parts of Alabama to participate in the Study, or other instances of deaths due to a spinal injury, Tammy's interpretation of the events illustrates a common sense of distrust among Black people, particularly those living in the Jim Crow South. Black people often lived with the threat of violence or meeting an untimely death, the circumstances of which may never have been made clear or fully acknowledged (Litwack, 1999; Reverby, 2001). In addition, it is possible that her great-grandfather underwent a botched spinal tap during the course of Study, which would explain his "spinal injury" or "broken back."

But for Tammy, the circumstances of her relative's death were less important than the deep vulnerability it caused her family. His death seemed to exemplify their exposure to trickery, deceit, and premature death. It also catalyzed a series of events that had a profound effect on multiple generations of her family, including Tammy's own children. For example, Tammy was mortally fearful of receiving an injection given by a White provider:

> You can't get a shot. I've never gotten a shot by a White person ever . . . they had me terrified [of being treated by a White doctor].

However, there is no evidence that the men in the Study were ever injected with syphilis. Rather, they were enrolled in the Study only if they already had the infection. In spite of this, the idea that Black men were purposely given syphilis persists,[7] and the imagery of needles and injections played a prominent role in Tammy's understanding of what happened to her great-grandfather and, by extension, what could happen to her.

Moreover, many of the Study's most disturbing details are not commonly known or appreciated. For example, at least in the early stages of the Study, the US government went to great lengths to ensure Study respondents could not inadvertently access treatment elsewhere (e.g., through other local physicians, mobile rapid treatment centers that were common in the 1940s and '50s, or through routine testing during the process of enlisting in the US Armed Services; Reverby, 2001). Researchers also subjected men to painful spinal taps, without the use of anesthetic, to determine the stage of syphilis, yet led the participants to believe that these taps were a form treatment (Jones, 1993), which may explain what happened to Tammy's great-grandfather. Particularly during the early years of the Study, conducting a spinal tap was a challenging and potentially life-threatening medical procedure (Reverby, 2012). Given that the men were obviously left in the dark about the risks of the Study overall, it follows that they were not told about this particular procedure as well.

---

[7] Although the men in the Tuskegee Study were not injected with syphilis, between 1946 and 1948 the USPHS did, in fact, deliberately infect nearly 700 Guatemalans, many of whom were prisoners, persons with mental illness, and soldiers. Prostitutes with syphilis were paid to have sex with prisoners to infect them. If that was unsuccessful, the researchers scraped the men's penises and then poured the bacteria onto the cuts. Other men were inoculated through spinal punctures. Dr. John C. Cutler, the man who led the Guatemala study, would go on to play a prominent role in the Tuskegee Study as well (McNeil, 2010).

The Study persisted for 40 years before a whistleblower was finally able to stop it.[8] But not before 40 women and their 19 children were infected through contact with their husbands and (through congenital exposure, respectively) (Brandt, 1978). Furthermore, although the record keeping was sometimes lax, it appears that at least 28 and perhaps up to 100 men died from syphilis or its complications (Brandt, 1978). And while so many may have died directly as a result of this study, no criminal charges were ever brought against the US government or individual researchers. Instead, the US government provided a $10 million out-of-court settlement to the men and their families, which amounted to approximately $37,500 per syphilitic man.[9] In other words, the men who suffered through the advanced stages of syphilis and its complications received approximately $937[10] per year of the Study. Even the acknowledgment of what the government had done to its own citizens was withheld until 1997, when then-President Bill Clinton delivered a formal apology to the men and their families. By then, most of the men were already deceased.

Against this backdrop, the word "preference" seems inadequate to describe Tammy's desire to control her healthcare experiences and presumably, by extension, to control her life. In many ways, Tammy's insistence on avoiding White healthcare providers is akin to a powerful assertion of her free will and humanity. Tammy was adamant that she exercise her preference for a Black provider. She recalled the exceptional care her African male ob-gyn took with her during the delivery of her first child:

> But I just wonder if the relationship I had with my doctors, and they know I value them because you know I look for certain doctors upfront. It's like I don't play because I need a Black doctor. If you want to put a needle anywhere near—if you want to be in a room with me and a needle, he needs to be Black, period. And I just think he took—he just took that extra time and that extra care with me and I think I benefitted in a way that a lot of girlfriends I know who had children since and all these cuts and C-sections and episiotomies and stuff don't.

[8] After years of demanding his employer, the Centers for Disease Control and Prevention, stop the Study, Peter Buxton eventually went to the press. The story broke in 1972, and the Study was stopped as a result (Rosenfeld, 1999).

[9] In the nomenclature of research methods, the Study was designed as a standard "treatment" versus "control" experiment in which men with syphilis (i.e., the treatment group) would be compared to men without syphilis (i.e., the controls). The term "treatment" group is used to denote that the men had syphilis even though the explicit purpose of the Study was to withhold medical treatment.

[10] In 1972 dollars, $937 had the same buying power as approximately $5,500 in 2017.

Tammy implied that she received more personal treatment from a Black (African) physician because they are both Black and that her friends who didn't insist on seeking such similarity may not have received such personal care. Tammy was not concerned about the nationality or gender of her physician. For her, being treated by a Black physician was more important than all other considerations. Tammy went on to elaborate on her feelings about seeking Black providers even in situations where it may be difficult to locate a Black provider:

> I would never let a White person touch me. I've been everywhere. I've been all over the world. My daughters' passports are well used. We've never been somewhere where there were no other Black people, no other Black professionals.... Definitely not White and probably another person of color. I would look at that the same way. But I haven't yet.
>
> I've been Black so far [meaning she has only seen Black providers thus far].

When other focus group respondents challenged her perspective, she revealed additional information:

> Like I said, my great-granddad was killed in the Tuskegee Experiment ... but the bigger thing is, after that, this Irish dude decided that my great-grandma was his girlfriend and had all these kids. So my family is biracial but not by choice. So . . . I have choices. You know everyone in my family has a choice that great-grandma didn't have, that my great-grandfather didn't have. So we all have those choices.

Tammy's comments, which she relayed with clear emotion in her voice, recall a legacy of trauma and victimization that reverberates in the present. Because her family members did not have many choices about healthcare, reproduction, or in general, Tammy vehemently exercised her agency to seek a Black provider and to support members of the Black community. Furthermore, it is important to situate her story in the larger context of the distrust and disenfranchisement Black people have labored under in the United States for centuries. Black people's distrust of the medical establishment is often interpreted as a disproportionate reaction to a single, albeit horrific, incident in the past. But the Tuskegee Study is not the only example of experimentation on Black Americans and other racial minorities.[11] African Americans are also well aware of substandard treatment

---

[11] For a thorough history of this topic, see Harriet A. Washington's *Medical Apartheid: The Dark History of Medical Experimentation on Black Americans from Colonial Times to the Present* (2006). African Americans are not the only group that has been experimented on by the US government.

in racially segregated hospitals and in medical care in general (Dittmer, 2017), and Tammy's family story demonstrates that the trauma of Tuskegee was clearly intertwined with other dehumanizing experiences that African Americans faced more generally, including the prevalence of sexual exploitation of Black women by White men (McGuire, 2010).

Later, during the follow-up interview I conducted with Tammy, she elaborated on her family's experience after her great-grandfather's death. She recalled that her great-grandmother went on to have nine children with the Irishman, but their relationship could never be formally acknowledged. Tammy also implied that the relationship was coercive and not completely consensual. Moreover, Tammy described her relatives' challenges living in the Jim Crow South in a family of mixed-race people, some of whom looked White while others did not:

> And so the way that my relatives look, that's not by choice. It's a very negative part of our family history. . . . And so my great-grandma, she ended up having a lot of land, and crops, and some cows, and whatever. We had some chickens and some hogs. And so by Southern means, she was kind of wealthy.
>
> But, my granddad, my grandma, my older aunts and uncles, they always said if there is a Black business, you go spend your money there 'cause nobody can tell you what to do with your money . . . because most of his sisters and brothers looked White, but they weren't White. And then some of them didn't look White. So, then being in town and you look White, it was actually kind of dangerous for them to be in the store because you had the Colored only, the Whites only [referring to the system of strict segregation of public spaces in the Jim Crow South].

Tammy goes on to explain the tightrope her family was forced to navigate because some members of the family appeared White but were not (at least according to the US conventional practice of hypo-descent[12]), which placed them in danger in a system of rigid public segregation,

In 2011, a study in the *Journal of Policy History* documented the US Public Health Service's experimentation on Guatemalan prisoners and mental patients who were purposely infected with syphilis between 1946 and 1948 (Reverby, 2011). Many ethically questionable practices (e.g., nonconsensual sterilization in the 1960s, prisoner research in the 1970s, and psychiatric research on Black and Latino children in the 1990s) continued until the recent past, and ethical lapses in research may continue unknown to the larger community (Washington, 2006).

[12] Hypo-descent, or the "one drop rule," refers to the American practice of categorizing someone with any phenotypical hint of Blackness as Black regardless of whether they appear predominantly European (Hollinger, 2003).

But, if you're not White, you can't use the Whites only. It was a very bad situation for everyone because the looking White, but not being White— so, you couldn't use either facility. You couldn't shop in either store. You just couldn't do anything. Or they couldn't go out with my relatives 'cause that can make my biracial-looking relatives—that could put them in danger.

And so at the Black stores, they could. It was safe. It was safe to have a Black service provider, buy at Black stores. It was just safe. And so I think that's where it started.

In this passage, Tammy seems to trace the evolution of her current "preference" for Black doctors as she noted that "safety" was the underlying motivation for her insistence on seeking out Black service providers. In this way, she emphasized the importance of the connection between events in the past (i.e., her great-grandfather's death and her great-grandmother's subsequent sexual exploitation and numerous mixed-race children) and her current conceptualization of "choice."

For example, Tammy also noted that during the birth of one of her children at a hospital in Chicago, she asked that no White men be present during the delivery. She explained that the hospital staff asked her to fill out a patient preference form:

And so they gave me a paper to ask whatever—what your preferences were. I don't know. It may have been something about religion. Who knows? But, you get a paper that says if you have some preferences about your healthcare, you can fill it out. And I said, "Well, I don't want a White man in my room." And my doctor said, "I understand." Some of the nurses were offended, but I didn't want it. And I said, "Is that a problem?" And my doctor said, "No." And the nurses were very uncomfortable that I didn't have a White man as a doctor in the room with me.

Later, when describing another event involving her then 11-year-old daughter, she discussed her regret over not believing the physician when he diagnosed her daughter with appendicitis.

Although Tammy was resolute throughout the interview, she lamented her decision to not allow her daughter to be treated by a White physician. She explained:

So I took her to the hospital because throwing up is just—I don't know. And the doctor said it was her appendix and I'm like, "No it wasn't. Let's do some more tests." And I feel so horrible about it now because he told me that at like 10:00 AM, and my baby didn't get her appendix taken out until like 7:00 PM because of my . . . [her voice trailed off]."

She went on to explain that she did not allow her daughter to have the emergency surgery until her husband arrived at the hospital and told the staff they needed to have a Black physician:

> And I'm a horrible patient because then I called my husband and he had to come and tell them that we needed somebody else who looked like I wanted them to tell me . . . and I just didn't want them to cut my child. And so, yeah, I just didn't want them—I didn't take what they told me, and it ended up being that. And they gave me a picture of her infected appendix—but I still made her wait all day and I feel horrible about that, but I just didn't believe the doctors. I just didn't believe them.

Tammy's distrust of the medical system was profound, and the fact that she refused consent to treatment for several hours distressed her as well. This situation seems to illustrate the kind of double bind Black people find themselves in between trying to hold the line on her wish to be treated by Black providers while simultaneously looking out for the best interest of her child. Although it may be obvious to others that her daughter's health may have been compromised, for Tammy, the alternative seemed just as dire. Tammy truly believed that, in this situation, she had a choice between two equally bad alternatives.

Understanding Tammy's decisions must be done in the broader context of how Black people have been treated by dominant institutions through time. As political scientist Cathy Cohen (1999) notes in her analysis of HIV/AIDS in the Black community, "feelings of alienation and distance result not from a one-time, or single-domain experience of marginalization, but instead are rooted in a historical experience of exclusion across domains" (p. 50). Cohen (1999) goes on to echo Tammy's distrust of the medical establishment: "it would be difficult to understand the current mistrust of the medical establishment exhibited by Black Americans without knowing the history of exploitation and blame that has been directed toward them under the guise of health and medicine" (p. 50).

Furthermore, Tammy's story points to the absurdity of America's rigid racial strictures that divided family members based on their racial phenotype. Although some members of her family appeared White because they had a White father, there was no possibility her family could formally acknowledge their lineage during this time period. The fact that the dominant society refused to recognize the coercive and often violent manner in which White men produced offspring with Black women should be considered tragedy enough. But, for Tammy's family, the implications seeped into the mundane tasks of life in which simply trying to go into a store with a relative who looked White but was not considered White could lead to violence. The day-to-day toll of these kinds of adaptations are typically omitted in health disparities research, but Tammy's story illustrates how past trauma ripples into the present.

In addition, the United States has long advanced the idea that Blacks and Whites were different biological beings that necessitated separate Black and White space. This idea actually laid the foundation for the Tuskegee Study, given that its purpose was to test the belief in essential biological differences between races. Tammy's story exposes the fundamental untruths of the American racial project particularly with regard to upholding the idea of race as a biological construct.

Finally, Tammy's experience highlights two important considerations for contemporary health inequity research. First, although Tammy's family history with the Tuskegee Study is distinctive, apart from the specifics of the Study many Black American families may share a similar history of uncertainty, vulnerability, and mistrust of predominately White institutions. In that respect, Tammy's case points to the durability of distrust in healthcare settings. Second, her contemporary "preference" for Black providers cannot be understood apart from the larger context of her family history. It is not simply a preference to be treated by a Black doctor, but a deep-seated concern born of multigenerational interactions with institutions that were beyond untrustworthy. In fact, engaging with these institutions may have cost people their lives. In Tammy's case, the word "preference" is inadequate to convey the underlying motivation of her decision to seek care from Black-only providers. It is rooted in an experience much bigger than healthcare, as evidenced by the multigenerational and multisetting consequences of her great-grandfather's death. Furthermore, as philosopher and social theorist Michel Foucault has cautioned us to consider "the history of the present," Tammy highlights the ongoing relevance of historic events to the contemporary moment (Foucault, 1977). At the conclusion of our interview, Tammy remarked, "People want to distance our *current* from our *past* and it's not that long ago." Indeed, Tammy illustrates the complexity and long reach of historical, collective traumas that cannot be overlooked.

Part 2

Do Black Middle-Class Women Prefer Black Doctors?

Although Tammy's story was deeply personal and powerful, other members of the focus group seemed uncomfortable with her point of view. In spite of the fact that they displayed great empathy toward her, they were incredulous that she would not be treated by a non-Black provider even in extremis. Contrary to the literature on race concordance among minority patients, the majority of women in this study did not uniformly support the idea that Black people prefer Black providers. In fact, many respondents, in both the interviews and focus groups, stated that the race of the provider was categorically unimportant to them. In contrast, a recent review of Black patients' medical adherence found less patient trust and adherence to treatment when the doctor was not Black (Hagiwara et al., 2013).

The provider's racial background was important to the women, but their opinions were more nuanced and conditional than much of the health disparities literature would suggest. Their comments reflected their experience in the world broadly, in which, after having providers of all races and ethnic backgrounds, they concluded that quality of care did not depend on the doctor's race. In addition, given that these data were collected in Chicago, it is possible that living in a large and racially diverse urban area required the women to come into contact with medical professionals of all backgrounds. Their preferences may have been shaped by the diversity of the racial and ethnic context of the Chicago healthcare market, which is not often explored in studies of race concordance.

As such, these data support a sophisticated interpretation of race preference. That is, in some instances, they expressed an affinity for Black providers but they did not necessarily prefer to be treated by them each time they see a healthcare provider.

For example, Sarah, a 40-year-old network manager with a health insurance company, noted that she had many experiences with providers of all racial and ethnic backgrounds:

> Well, my cardiologist, he's a White man. My son's pediatrician is an Indian man. I've had Filipino doctors . . . the pediatrician I fell in love with, she was a Black woman. So to me, I don't really care what your race is, as long as you're not my gynecologist you can be a man. And as long as you're willing to talk with me and work with me and you're a good doctor, then I can deal with them. That's the most important thing to me.

Ellen, a 60-year-old IT salesperson, echoed Sarah's sentiments:

> Well, except for one resident that I met, all of my doctors are White. And I've always been able to relate one-on-one with people . . . and this is so interesting because a lot of times when I talk to my mother she will ask me, "Are they White?" And I have to think about it before I answer because I don't think about color first.

I think about: are you a good person? Are you who I need in my
life? And I wouldn't care if you were purple with pink polka dots. "If
you can do what I need or I want, I don't give a," as I call it, "a flying flip
on a rolling donut, as long as you and I can get me where I need to go."
So no, I don't think there is—I have not felt discrimination
because of color.

Ellen's comments reflect a particular strand of the American "colorblind" discourse in which "not seeing color" is upheld as an important social value. She
prided herself on being able to relate to people one on one and reflected on her
mother's emphasis on the racial background of the people with whom her daughter interacted. Ellen's perspective is interesting given that she grew up in the Jim
Crow South where she was one of a group of students to integrate an Alabama
high school, an experience she described as painful. She also attended a historically Black university that propelled her into action as a Civil Rights activist. She
reflected on her attitudes about race and gender over time and noted that when
she was in her 20s she wanted a female gynecologist but, because she could not
find one, she considered a Black male provider to be the next best thing:

> Now my ob-gyn when I was living in Washington, DC, was male, but
> he was Black, and that was another conscious decision because, at that
> time, way back then, I could not find a female ob-gyn. And I said, "But
> if I can't get a female I will get a Black person," because, again, perhaps
> he could relate more to the experience at the time.

Although at that point in her life, Ellen believed she would have more connection with another Black person, as she got older, her preferences softened, perhaps as a result of the vastly different meaning of "race" in the contemporary
United States. First, Ellen noted that her preference was shaped by a structural
constraint: In the 1960s, there simply were not many Black female physicians.
Therefore, although she may have preferred a Black woman, this option was simply not available to her so she chose the next best option based on her criteria: a
Black male physician. Ellen's comments illustrate that "preferences" are shaped
by what is possible. In other words, although the idea of race and gender preferences in healthcare settings are frequently discussed as though they are an individual property of the patient, they are undoubtedly influenced by the supply of
available physicians in the healthcare system. Therefore, I argue that the concept
of preference should consider the healthcare structure overall.

Second, Ellen lived in Washington, DC, during the 1960s, at the height of
intense political and social upheaval. Her choices were likely shaped by this
context. However, when I interviewed her in 2011, during the first Obama

administration, post-racialism had been advanced and celebrated by journalists, intellectuals, and other cultural leaders. The election of the nation's first Black (mixed-race) president supposedly signaled the end of the United States' centuries old struggle against structural racism. For Ellen, both her perspective and the context of her life had shifted substantively, which suggests that race and gender preferences are probably about individual choice, context, and the supply of available providers.

However, both Ellen and Sarah implied that the most important element of the healthcare encounter was being able to have a cooperative working relationship, something that is much more elusive than it should be in American healthcare. Ellen in particular emphasized her ability to relate to people individually, which harkened back to her comments about the importance of developing a personal connection with providers.[13] For both women, developing the foundation for a trusting working relationship was not necessarily predicated on sharing the same racial background.

Like Ellen and Sarah, another study participant highlighted the inherent flaws in the US system. Shelly, a 53-year-old real estate agent, felt that time pressure and the necessity to move patients quickly through the healthcare visit, was more salient than race concordance in determining quality of care. Shelly was a striking and dignified woman who commanded attention and respect. She and her husband had owned a home and raised their children in Geneva,[14] one of Chicago's most exclusive, wealthiest, and Whitest suburbs. Geneva's homes each sit on several acres of land, and many Geneva-ites own horses and stables. Just like the land, wealth and access were abundant in Geneva. But Black people were not. In spite of being one of a handful of Black families, Shelly had described Geneva as a real community in which she received excellent medical care. She attributed the excellent care she received to the fact that the community numbered fewer than 9,000 people and that, even before Yelp and Google, physician reviews spread like wildfire through word of mouth. As a result, physicians knew they had to treat people with dignity lest they build a negative reputation for themselves.

After her children left home, she sold her house in the suburbs and relocated to the city, taking a job at one of Chicago's largest and most prominent real estate firms. I interviewed her in her office and immediately noticed her perfect clothes, perfect brows, and a perfect pixie haircut framing a fine-boned face. Like

[13] Ellen strongly endorsed the importance of developing a personal connection with her provider and emphasized the importance of getting the provider to see you as an individual and not just another number. To be seen as an individual, and to treat others as such, seems to be part of her worldview.

[14] To maintain the respondent's privacy, I am using a pseudonym for the name of the town.

Ellen, Shelly did not seem to suffer fools gladly, and, when asked if she preferred a Black healthcare provider, she quickly dismissed the notion saying,

> [S]trangely enough, I don't . . . that doesn't make a difference.

Curious to know more, I asked whether her experiences with healthcare varied by race of provider.

> No. No, I really don't, as sad as that is, no—or maybe not sad. I just really think it's a broken system, because I've had White doctors, Black doctors, female, male, you know, just . . . I think there's not the personal concern. I think that people—I think that doctors in general—and there's the whole healthcare system—the incentive is to just keep them moving. Get 'em in, get 'em out, make as much money as possible. I don't think that there's really an incentive to find out what's wrong, and to just really give well care, and that the whole thing is geared toward emergency and crisis.

For Shelly, the most salient aspect of her experience was being rushed, not being listened to, and being treated as though she were just a commodity. Shelly touched on the emphasis on making money and moving people in and out quickly to increase profits. Her comments echoed those of other respondents who expressed great displeasure with the healthcare system's impersonal orientation to patients and the lack of comprehensive wellness care. In Shelley's experience, it was ridiculous to think that having a Black doctor could mitigate the financial and time pressures that are built into the American healthcare system overall.

Other women I encountered shared a similar perspective on the time pressure that characterizes the contemporary healthcare environment:

> But the biggest advocate for any of us is ourselves. If you're not being treated right, it's really up to you to act on what you feel and to find a better person. When I found a doctor who was in the group that I was in, I didn't care for that particular doctor; couldn't talk to him. He was watching his watch the whole time, trying to allot you your 15 minutes. He was not the one for me, and you can change only once a year the facility, but you can change each month the doctor. And I went on and changed.
>
> Focus group respondent

In contrast to Shelly, this woman was pleased with the quality of care she received. However, her comments reflect an important development in the American healthcare environment: the rise of patient consumerism and self-advocacy. Historian Nancy Tomes (2016) traces the ascendance of the "health-care consumer" to the early 20th century, when skeptical lay people first began to question medical authority in American society. To push back against the supposed omniscience of physicians, dissatisfied patients began to refer to themselves as "consumers" in an effort to emphasize their own power relative to their doctors. However, as Tomes argues in her 2016 take on American medical practice, *Remaking the American Patient: How Madison Avenue and Modern Medicine Turned Patients into Consumers*, the tension between financial business interests and medical professionalism has always hounded the healthcare industry. Tomes (2016) argues that American healthcare practices reveal growing tensions in modern American life: "The elevation of individualism and personal autonomy on the one hand, and deference to scientific expertise and authority on the other" (p. 10). She attributes the growth of these tensions to American reliance on neo-liberalism, which emphasizes the power of individuals to act in free markets.

In keeping with Tomes analysis of American healthcare, the women in both the interviews and focus groups emphasized the importance of self-advocacy, which in this respondent's case meant exercising her ability to get a second opinion. They also voiced their general displeasure with the way healthcare providers quickly process patients without giving sufficient time or care to individual needs. Taken together, their comments point to problems that are inherent to the healthcare system overall. At least in the mind's eye of many of the women, the pressure to see more and more patients cannot be mitigated by having a Black doctor.

Another focus group respondent encapsulated many of these themes:

> The one I have right now, my primary, I go and tell her what I'm dealing with. I've had male doctors, I've had Caucasian doctors, male, female. I don't check color. Color means nothing to me. If they listen to me and act on me . . . I know my body better than any doctor could. . . . I'm not coming in pushy, but I came to tell you I have a problem, and this is what's going on and we go from there.
>
> But I think you should walk in and present yourself to the doctor and not present a guessing game that they have to ask you 20 questions to pull out of you the reason you are there. If there is a problem, if you even think it's a problem, check it out.

Importantly, this woman emphasized the importance of one's cultural health capital, specifically her skill at digesting medical information, taking an instrumental approach to her own body, and having the verbal acumen to present the information back to the physician in a cogent and coherent way. She also reflects the healthcare industry's preoccupation with patient consumerism and self-advocacy. Instead of placing the locus of responsibility on the healthcare provider, the woman has internalized the notion of self-advocacy. Certainly, being in tune with yourself and being able to deliver complex health information to your physician is a good thing. However, I would argue that the overemphasis on patient (or self-) advocacy and consumerism may unwittingly place too much responsibility on the patient and not enough on providers and healthcare institutions.

Moreover, for Black women who are often viewed through the lens of the angry Black woman stereotype, asserting one's agency may not have the effect these women may have intended. Health services scholar Jennifer Malat has noted that while some physicians may view Black women positively if they are assertive during the healthcare visit, others may perceive them as aggressive (Malat, van Ryn, & Purcell, 2006). We simply do not know enough about how providers interpret self-advocacy among women who are perceived in the context of pervasive negative stereotypes. However, we know that the vigilance and repeated self-regulatory behaviors required to maneuver through racialized social spaces may lead to poor health, including hypertension and depression (Lee & Hicken, 2016).

Part 3

Power and Struggle Within the Black Community: Is Seeing a Black Doctor Enough?

Although the majority of women did not express a firm preference for a Black provider, several women discussed particularly positive relationships with Black female doctors.

Particularly for members of the Black middle class who may spend much of their time in predominantly White spaces, their comments suggest an affinity Black people often feel in the presence of other Black people, especially other Black women. However, this affinity must be understood in the context of existing intraracial fissures within the Black community. As Cathy Cohen posits, although Black people have less power than White people, there are varying degrees of power among Black people, and the variation typically falls along class, color, gender, and other dimensions. These fissures may lead to tension and miscommunication, as was the case with two respondents who had very negative experiences with Black female providers. The following section explores both the positive relationships, in which having a Black provider provided a sense of comfort and ease, as well as those that led to ruptures and miscommunication.

Connection

Leona, the 59-year-old divorced mother described in Chapter 2, was a frequent flyer at the doctor's office. Leona had polio as a child and suffered from post-polio syndrome, which left her paralyzed from the waist down. In spite of her disability, Leona performed in, and led, a dance company for able-bodied and disabled dancers. As a result of her condition, Leona had more contact with the medical profession than she would have liked, and her experience as a disabled, Black older woman was complex. Although she did not explicitly prefer Black female providers, she conveyed great pleasure when telling me about her new doctor:

> My ob-gynie is a Black female. Love her. Love her. She's new to me because my regular ob-gynie retired, and I got a referral and she came highly recommended and I—really, really like her.
>
> . . . Her bedside manner. She's so thorough, and she does give you that extra, you know what I mean? I feel so comfortable talking to her, even about the most awkward subjects. Yeah. I really like her.
>
> I feel like she relates to me at my current age, I feel like she relates to me as a Black woman, I feel like she relate—I respect her knowledge as a doctor, and I respect her candor and just the way she makes you feel so comfortable about bringing anything to her without judgment. Because I could talk to her about things that aren't totally medically related, and she's—yeah, so. I wish I had met her years ago.

Leona's felt a certain level of comfort with her new doctor because she could understand the multidimensionality of being an older Black woman who is also disabled. Unlike the other women in the study who expressed great frustration with rushed healthcare encounters, Leona implied that she was not rushed through her appointments and that the doctor was more thorough as a result. She was confident of the doctor's ability and level of personal closeness and connection. Although Leona was not particularly concerned about having a Black female doctor, her comments suggest that the comfort and ease she experienced with this particularly provider may not be possible with providers of other backgrounds. Moreover, Leona was an older, disabled Black woman, a member of a group that is often overlooked, both at the doctor's office and in research.

Leona's experience highlights the intersection of race, gender, disability, and age, which is often ignored in race disparities research but certainly affects the interaction between patient and provider. Leona also lamented that she did not encounter this physician previously, which may be an indication of the relative shortage of Black female physicians. As a result, while many women may prefer a Black female doctor, given the relative dearth of them in the medical field, they just do not expect to encounter many Black female doctors.

Sarah, a 40-year-old single woman and network manager at a health insurance company, also recounted a similarly close experience with her son's doctor, a Black female pediatrician.

> She was wonderful. I fell in love with her. And I switched within the same practice. So I just liked her so much better. I felt much more connected with her. . . . She was beautiful. She was gorgeous. She's Black. She's intelligent. Christian. I mean, she would pray. I mean, how sweet is that? "Let's just say a prayer." And she just loved this little baby, and she just took such good care of him. And she didn't dismiss me. And if I'd say, "This is really not working" or "I need to try something else" or "we need something a little stronger," she worked with me and I loved her, and then she left the practice.

In this instance, the pediatrician was particularly interested in Sarah's son's care and took extra time to respond to Sarah's concern about his speech acquisition. Sarah noted that the doctor did not dismiss her concerns and that their relationship was highly collaborative. Again, Sarah did not express a preference for a Black provider, nor did she specifically attribute her connection to the physician's race or gender. However, as Sarah lists the attributes she values in the provider, her race and religiosity were clearly important. Religiosity is highly valued among some segments of the Black community and is another factor that is often overlooked in research on the patient–provider relationship (Barnes, Plotnikoff, Fox, & Pendleton, 2000; Chandler, 2010; Giger, Appel, Davidhizar, & Davis, 2008). Furthermore, I would argue that although establishing a religious connection with a provider is not necessarily predicated on racial concordance, the conversation about religion is probably more likely to arise in an intraracial interaction. In that sense, although Sarah's sense of connection is not about race per se, the religious connection is likely a marker of shared cultural values.

Sarah's effusive praise of her son's pediatrician, and the fact that she clearly valued her because she was a Christian Black woman, appeared to contradict the fact that when I asked her if she had preferences, she stated that she did not. However, Sarah's comments throughout the interview, as well as those of other respondents, presented a fuller picture of how she thought about her healthcare experiences overall. First, Sarah's account of the majority of her healthcare providers is best described as glowing, regardless of the person's race. When asked about her current internist, who was a White woman, Sarah said, "I love her. It's a woman. She is so smart. And she's very practical. She listens to me. She's just really, really smart." Her evaluation of her other healthcare providers contained similarly glowing language in which she often said she "loved" the provider and then described their good qualities.

Second, because Sarah was a network manager for a large health insurance company, her insider knowledge of healthcare indelibly shaped her view of the quality of individual healthcare providers, which in turn led her to carefully research and choose physicians. Sarah stated:

> I would definitely categorize myself as an informed consumer of healthcare services. And also I think, being in insurance, because that's my field and what I've done since I've been working, it kind of takes away that kind of godlike presence that physicians have.
>
> You know they're people just like you and I, so there's no intimidation really for me personally.
>
> I'm one of those people who will go and look them up [referring to doctors] and see where they went to medical school and are there any malpractice suits against them. I check all that stuff, I do. I can't help it, I do. I know too many bad docs. They're people. And guess what, they're alcoholics and they have other criminal things going on. They are people.

Given her first-hand knowledge of physicians' limitations, it is not surprising that Sarah did not necessarily prefer a Black doctor. Sarah suggested that because there is great quality variation among physicians, the race of the provider is not an accurate criterion for assessing the physician's competency or likelihood of securing quality treatment.

However, Sarah was never sheepish about acknowledging racial discrimination, nor did she uphold the colorblind ethos that had reemerged in the United States during the Obama years. She had grown up during a very racially charged time in a neighborhood on Chicago's southwest side that was once a working-class Irish Catholic enclave. Black families who moved into the area in search of larger homes and better schools were frequently met with physical violence and intimidation. Given this experience, it was hard for Sarah to believe in the rhetoric of a post-racial America. However, she both valued the sense of cultural affinity she enjoyed with her son's pediatrician and was comfortable—and often very pleased—with providers of all racial and ethnic backgrounds. Sarah valued the connection she had with her Black female provider but also implied that all physicians are individuals who must be evaluated based on their own merit.

Sarah's view of racial concordance encapsulates many of the same themes expressed by other respondents: they have had specific instances of connection with Black providers, but they do not necessarily prefer one racial background across the board.

Sarah's and Leona's comments suggest that Black women feel some level of comfort with Black providers, which probably facilitates communication during the healthcare visit. The feeling of comfort upholds the underlying assumptions upon which the race concordance hypothesis rests. Another woman named Marie, who participated in a focus group with other lower middle-class women, recalled an experience with a Black male physician who took her deep fatigue seriously and insisted on asking further questions about how she felt. She explained:

> There were some cultural—the reason I got to him [referring to a specialist] is I told my doctor, who was an African American physician, that, you know what, I'm so tired. It's too hard to carry my coat. He said, "Marie, come back in my office." He heard me from a cultural perspective and from a knowledge of understanding Black women don't complain unless they have something, especially about something minute. So the whole situation of me not being able to carry out a routine activity without being fatigued caused me to get an exam. I was on my way even out of his door when he—when I made that statement.

In this situation, Marie did not demonstrate the kind of cultural health capital skills that seem to be a prerequisite in the contemporary healthcare environment. She did not present her condition in the cogent, rational manner that is often demanded by rushed and impersonal interactions with providers. Instead, Marie commented on her deep fatigue in an offhanded manner, as though she did not expect the provider to follow-up. But, at least for Marie, the fact that her physician asked her to come back into the office to investigate further was an indication that he understood there was something wrong and that he cared enough to ask about it. Marie interpreted the interaction as an example of a cultural knowledge that would not have been possible without that shared connection with her doctor.

Taken together, Marie's, Sarah's, and Leona's comments point to an underlying construct of familiarity that comes from a shared background. Although none of these women expressed a strong preference for a Black provider, their comments suggest that, in terms of facilitating communication and comfort, having a Black doctor may be beneficial. Also, in Marie's case, the sense of ease led to a material outcome: being referred to a specialist for additional workup. The absence of this kind of understanding or empathy may explain, in part, why the US healthcare system continues to struggle with differences in treatment, including those that persist across class. In other words, if Marie, and other women like her, did not have the benefit of a doctor who understood and empathized with her, she may never have received the referral to the specialist and her health may have declined. The empathy and subtlety of this interaction may have quite literally saved her life.

However, perhaps because there are so many factors women are likely to look for in a physician, from access to certain specialists and subject matter expertise, the doctor's race may not be prioritized very highly, particularly in an overall healthcare context that is rushed, impersonal, and crisis-oriented. Although Black women may feel a certain comfort with Black doctors that facilitates communication and cooperation, the supply of Black female physicians may be insufficient.

Misrecognition

The underlying premise of the race concordance hypothesis is that Black people are necessarily more comfortable with other Black people than they would be with non-Black people. Taking the argument a step further, the hypothesis implies that the connection between Black people is based on a cultural shorthand (e.g., not having to explain why you eat certain foods or care for your hair a particular way). However, the essence of the connection many Black women feel with other Black people may also lead to misunderstandings and misrecognition based on deeply rooted hierarchies within the Black community (e.g., skin color, weight, and class). As Cohen and other scholars have theorized, there are undoubtedly fissures within the Black community that may manifest themselves in healthcare settings. These factors have particular salience between Black people, and, while they may enjoy a kind of cultural shorthand with each other, sorting based on color and class may be uncomfortable or downright painful. Moreover, as I have argued throughout the book, the politics of respectability, particularly for the Black middle class, may have poisoned Black people's relationships with each other. That is to say, given the emphasis on proper comportment and positive self-presentation, it is hardly surprising that these tropes may be internalized and used by members of the Black community against other Black people.

Bobbi's experience with her Black female ob-gyn illustrates the intraracial tension that may strain the patient–provider relationship. At the time of the interview, Bobbi was a 46-year-old single woman who worked in the financial services industry. She made well over $100,000 a year and lived in a fashionable and predominantly White neighborhood on the Northside. As I drove to her townhouse near Wrigley Field, I was struck by the marked shift in the people and the landscape as the expressway curved around the ball park in Chicago White Sox territory on the Southside to Cubs Country on the Northside. As I climbed the stairs to her home, I wondered how she experienced living in this neighborhood. Was she friendly with the neighbors? Did they walk to Wrigley together to catch night games? At any rate, when she opened the door, I was struck by her small stature and muscular frame. As she would later tell me, her physical fitness and slight build played an important role in her healthcare experience.

Bobbi was gracious enough to invite a stranger into her home on a Sunday afternoon even while she was fasting in preparation for a medical procedure the following day. Throughout the interview, we both ignored the low rumblings of her growling stomach. She seemed to be a person who was used to being in control of her life, and this day was no different; growling stomach or not, she pressed on to tell me what it was like to be a financially successful Black woman in the predominately White world of finance.

Bobbi told me that she initially sought out a Black woman ob-gyn because she wanted to support a Black doctor and because the particular physician she chose had been recommended by a Latina colleague. According to Bobbi, the physician's practice comprised many Black and Latina women, which Bobbi felt was because the women believed they would receive better care from a minority female physician.

> She's a Black doctor, and a lot of Black and Hispanic people go to her— her waiting room is just thick with Black and Hispanic women who are hanging on her every word . . . they probably falsely believe that they're gonna get a better quality of care because she is African American.

Bobbi's feelings about the provider were conflicted throughout their relationship, but they came to a head over the physician's hasty recommendation that she have a hysterectomy for a single uterine fibroid. Bobbi was upset with the provider's callous interpersonal skills and disregard for their long-term relationship. Bobbi's interpretation of events pointed to the subtleties of an intraracial relationship that is theoretically supposed to facilitate communication or a sense of ease, but, like other relationships, having the same racial background does not necessarily lead to understanding.

Nonetheless, Bobbi (who was 43 at the time) was told she had a single uterine fibroid, and, without further discussion, her doctor recommended a hysterectomy. After an initial diagnostic procedure in which the physician had the

opportunity to remove the fibroid, the physician left without discussing the outcome with Bobbi:

> After I come out of surgery, she's not there. She's gone. She's gone, she
> leaves after surgery, and my uncle was there.
>
> So she's gone, and so my uncle is there. My uncle was the one
> who took me to the hospital. He tells me, "She didn't take it out." It's,
> like, what?
>
> She's not there to tell. I call her on her phone, and she's upset that
> I call her on her phone. [Laughing] She's upset that I would even dare
> call her.
>
> And so, "I will talk to you when I'm in my office. Make an appoint-
> ment." Yeah, okay? So I make an appointment, go see her. "You need a
> hysterectomy."
>
> Yeah. "You need a hysterectomy," and I'm just in shock when some-
> body says that. Do you know what her response to me was? "Are you
> gonna cry or something?" Yes.
>
> I said, "Fine." I walked out of her office. I was just upset. I was pissed,
> and I was—literally, I walked from Rush [a hospital several miles from
> downtown] back downtown, 'cause I just lost it.

The interaction with this physician could be described as callous or completely lacking empathy. The physician did not wait to consult with Bobbi after
the surgery, and she seemed to taunt her about her reaction to the progno-
sis. The physician's interpersonal skills would surely be described as coarse or
almost cruel.

Bobbi eventually sought treatment from a White male physician who dis-
agreed with the previous doctor's recommendation that she needed a hysterectomy. In Bobbi's retelling of the story, she was particularly upset that the
physician recommended "taking an organ out of my body" without providing the proper context or alternative treatment options. In retrospect, she was
also annoyed that she was often required to wait for long periods to see the
doctor, even with an appointment. She likened the experience to waiting in
a Black hair salon, a trope among Black women. For example, although there
are few scholarly accounts of wait times in Black hair salons, there are numerous pop cultural references to the frustration Black women experience at both
having to wait long hours to receive relatively simple hair care services *and*
being expected to wait excessively (8–9 hours plus) without complaining
(King, 2016). Although waiting to get your hair done may seem trivial, Bobbi
explains her frustration:

I wish I would have found a better—a doctor sooner, because just the waiting—when I look back on it, she would—even if you took—even if you had the 8:00 appointment, she would schedule four people at 8:00. I mean, that's—it was just like going to a Black hairdresser. It's just—it's the same thing.

I didn't get that., now when I go to Dr. Keller's office, if I have to wait a long time, they'll say, "Oh, no, Dr. Keller was running behind. It may be a 45-minute wait." They tell me up front and she would expect me to sit there. I have actually got to her office and the office door wasn't even open, and we were waiting for the nurses . . . if this is something you're kind of used to, you know how you don't realize it could be different. And as soon as you leave that environment, you're, like, wow, it really is different.

It doesn't—I don't have to be treated like that. I don't have to—just for—you know, I'm paying you. I don't—I shouldn't have to be treated like that. So I really wish I would have got out of the situation earlier.

Bobbi went on to explain the sense of racial solidarity and conflict she felt over leaving a Black doctor to seek care from a White male physician:

That I had to wait to a critical point and have a very bad experience with her before I actually would seek out another doctor. Because you do, you want to patronize a Black doctor. You want to—you know, so you kind of feel guilty.

I feel guilty. Yeah, I feel badly, because I felt that I was turning my back on my own kind. You know, you want to patronize people, but, you know, especially I think it's hard—I'm sure it was hard for her to build her practice, and I think that's the part—that's part of why I haven't submitted any sort of complaint, is because you feel bad for her.

You know, you don't want to see her—I don't want to see her career, you know, decimated, but I think that the way I was treated was just—it was egregious.

Bobbi's comments point to a different underlying motivation for seeking the care of a Black doctor. While the race concordance hypothesis suggests Black people prefer a Black doctor because of common cultural understandings that improve the patient–provider relationship, Bobbi's motivation was to lend financial and professional support to another Black woman. Bobbi grew up outside Detroit at a time in which many Black people did not receive professional degrees, and she endured a racially hostile environment while getting her bachelor's degree at a state university in Michigan. Moreover, as a result of her own experience in the corporate world, Bobbi was well aware of how difficult it could be for Black women to establish professional careers. Her comments throughout the interview indicated a conflict between her desire to support the Black community and the sense of rejection she felt from other Black people. When asked specifically if she felt being a Black woman affected the quality of her healthcare she responded:

> Yeah, but I think it has hindered me with other Black people. With White people, it's not a problem. It's been more a problem, because before—I remember a gynecologist I had a long time ago. She was a Black woman, because I went to another Black woman before I went to Dr. Bowman [pseudonym]. I don't remember her name. She was nasty to me, too. She was very nasty to me. And so I've had better treatment from the Caucasian people—or the non-African American people I've gone to than her.
>
> Because when I go to a White doctor, I don't feel that—I don't feel that they look at me as Black and I'm gonna give you less care.
>
> No, I do not think my White doctors do. I think my Black doctors did, though.

When I asked her to explain why, she noted:

> Probably because of the color of my skin, because I'm lighter complected, because I am educated, because I can speak up, and I am going to take a little bit more action and be a little bit more forthright in fighting for my healthcare. It could be a turnoff that I'm questioning them or maybe because I'm smaller or thinner or lighter, that there, somehow there is, you know, I don't like you. I'm not gonna do this—these things for you.
>
> Because a lot—you know, you probably feel it, too [referring to myself, who is also lighter complected]. You know, you go around darker complected Black people and they will say—make various snide comments . . . "Who do you think you are?" And it's that whole, you know, house nigger mentality. You know, I had to be a field nigger, you're a house nigger, so things are better for you.

Although Bobbi initially sought a Black female physician, presumably to support another Black woman, her experience was soured by the conflicts that arise between Black people.

Bobbi's experience touches on long-simmering issues within the Black community around skin color and class, and she acknowledges the ways in which being lighter skinned is associated with being middle-class. The idea that having a lighter complexion confers certain benefits to Black people in general and Black women in particular is a source of great tension in the Black community. For example, sociologist Maxine Leeds Craig (2009) notes in her essay, "The Color of an Ideal Negro Beauty Queen," "class and color were often intertwined and provided a readily available frame for Black women to understand their experiences" (p. 93). Furthermore, color, hair texture, and body type are all elements in a system of race, gender, and class within the Black community that mark Black women's social position. Importantly, these valuations of lightness, slimness, and "middle class–ness" did not just emerge within the Black community out of nowhere. Rather, they are an expression of racist and gendered systems of representation in that Blacks often see themselves and judge themselves as Whites see them (Cohen, 1999; Leeds Craig, 2009). As such, Bobbi understands that, on the one hand, she is relatively advantaged within the Black community because she is a slim, light-skinned, well-educated, professional woman who approximates a White standard of beauty. On the other hand, she also understands that, among Black people, darker skin often signifies authenticity while light skin is associated with a lack of credibility and privilege (Leeds Craig, 2009).

Obviously, I am privileging Bobbi's interpretation of events, but it is telling that Bobbi experienced these tensions with at least one other Black female doctor. Bobbi eventually decided to "break up" with her doctor even though she was conflicted over her decision to leave a Black female doctor to seek the care of a White male physician. In spite of the inherent conflict in her interactions with Black providers, Bobbi's experience is absent from the discussion of race concordance as a strategy to reduce health inequities. This relationship, and others like it, suggests that the healthcare system should not erase the complexities of intraracial relationships. One would certainly not expect all White people to get along with their physicians simply because the physician was also White. Interventions to address racial inequities in healthcare should take the same sophisticated and nuanced approach to Black people as well.

Part 4

"It's Just Like Going to a Black Hairdresser": Healthcare Facilities and Black Doctors

> I wish I would have found a better—a doctor sooner, because just the waiting—when I look back on it, she would—even if you took—even if you had the 8:00 appointment, she would schedule four people at 8:00. I mean, that's—it was just like going to a Black hairdresser. It's just—it's the same thing.
>
> —Bobbi, 46, finance executive

Bobbi's negative experience with her ob-gyn was obviously a conflict between two individuals. We do not know her physician's side of the story, but it is certainly possible that her view of the relationship would differ from Bobbi's. However, although we typically consider race and gender preferences at the individual level (i.e., occurring between two people), Bobbi's story suggests that preferences for individual providers may be shaped by perceptions of the healthcare facility overall. In other words, Bobbi, and other study participants, described the site-level factors that affected their preference, including having to wait a long time to see their doctor, the racial composition of other patients at the site, and interpersonal treatment from allied/support staff in the healthcare facility. Although much of the health services research focuses on the interactions between the patient and provider, many women suggested that their preferences for Black providers are shaped by what having a Black doctor means for the healthcare facility overall.

For example, Bobbi's situation raises the question of whether preference for a Black provider is conflated with the culture of the overall practice and the racial and socioeconomic composition of the patients in particular. Women may feel that being treated at a predominately Black site brings an additional level of burdens (e.g., long wait times, shoddy interpersonal treatment from support staff, lower quality amenities, etc.).

Research in other domains of African American life, particularly housing and neighborhoods, may help us understand Black people's racial preferences in healthcare. For example, on average, Black people express a greater preference (compared to their White counterparts) to live in racially integrated neighborhoods in which half the residents are Black and half are White or Latino (Havekes, Bader, & Krysan, 2016). Furthermore, Black people with more education are less likely to want to live in a majority Black neighborhood than those with less education (Pattillo, 2005). We also know that, at all levels of income, Black people live in neighborhoods with fewer institutional amenities compared to White people. And that Black middle-class neighborhoods are often contiguous with poorer, higher crime neighborhoods with a high proportion of Black residents (Lee & Hughes, 2015; Pattillo, 2005). If we extend this logic to healthcare, it is possible that African Americans associate a higher proportion of minority and lower income patients with lower quality treatment. We know that many aspects of American life remain "separate and unequal" (Alexander, 2010). Therefore, it is hardly surprising that African Americans may use the race-of-provider as a proxy for the racial and socioeconomic composition of the practice, which in turn is a proxy for lower quality amenities and poorer overall treatment. As a result, Black people, and particularly members of the Black middle class who have the resources to do so, may seek providers in sites with a more diverse patient mix, better site-level amenities, and shorter wait times.

Like Bobbi, Veronica was not alone in her frustration with the practice style of Black providers. Veronica was a 47-year-old IT executive for a school system whom I interviewed in a famous soul food restaurant on the Southside. She described long waits and unpleasant interpersonal treatment that would chafe a person with very little to do, let alone a professional woman with little free time. For example, Veronica described a 4-hour wait at the office of her long-time primary care doctor:

> Now my primary care physician, the last time I went I think I had a 2:00 appointment. I got in there at 6:00 and I let him have it. Yes, yes, yes. He's like, "Veronica, when you come that's the only days I'm late." I'm like, "You're lying, Dr. Nigel [pseudonym], you're lying."
>
> But again, it's kind of like a joking relationship 'cause I know. I brought something to eat. I brought my laptop. I brought some work, you know. So I knew I was gonna be there all day. But I think that's a symptom of the plan. He belongs to a lot of plans. He's in a lot of plans. So I don't know why. I don't know if it's something on his end where he gets paid for doing so much of this, that, or the other, but actually his nurses, he'll have a 9:30 appointment in the morning, and I know Dr. Nigel doesn't get in until 10:00. I know that. So why does he have a 9:00? He'll have a 9:00 and a 9:30. So he starts his day already behind. So I have no idea. And if he really was not my family physician I'd probably go somewhere else.

Veronica's preparation for the visit, which included bringing food and her laptop, indicated that she had adapted to Dr. Nigel's practice style over time. Because she was a busy woman with a senior position in the public school system, she could not afford to lose that much time at the doctor's office but she accepted waiting because he had been the family doctor for years. She felt his personal knowledge of her family's health history outweighed the excessive wait times. Importantly, Veronica did not say she preferred Black providers, nor did she believe her own healthcare treatment was negatively affected by being a Black woman. However, she noted that her commitment to their long-standing relationship was more important than her frustration with his tardiness.

Taken together, Veronica's and Bobbi's experiences raise important questions about Black people's evaluation of race preference. For example, is Bobbi's vehement avoidance of Black providers explained by the individual provider, or is it connected to her perception of the level of service provided in a majority Black practice? Do middle-class Black people perceive poorer quality service when the patient composition reaches a certain racial and socioeconomic tipping point? If so, how do we interpret this finding?

Although these data do not allow me to conclusively answer these questions, they suggest some important points. First, it appears that when asked explicitly, the study participants did not necessarily prefer Black providers. However, they undoubtedly have a certain affinity with other Black people, which, in certain cases, results in a more pleasant healthcare experience. This may explain why quantitative studies of race concordance have been mixed (Shen et al., 2017; Sweeney et al., 2016). But this affinity cannot override structural discrimination. Second, race preferences seem to operate at both the individual provider level and the healthcare facility level. As such, respondents may have preferences for both the provider and the practice, including the allied and support staff and the patient racial composition. However, because people's healthcare needs and the healthcare system are so complex, it may deter women from even expressing these preferences or trying to act on them.

Part 5

"Ain't I a Woman?": Black Women's Gender Preferences in Healthcare Settings

So it doesn't really matter if they were Black or White, Asian, whatever.
As long as they were a woman.
—Gillian, 53, sales coordinator at a real estate firm

Although health disparities research emphasizes increasing the proportion of Black patients treated by Black providers to reduce differences in treatment, little attention is paid to how minority women think about how race *and* gender affect them at the doctor's office (Casciotti & Klassen, 2011).[15] This is hardly surprising given the relative lack of attention to the intersectional effects of race and gender for women who are not White (Choo & Ferree, 2010; Crenshaw, 1991). However, although most of the women in this study did not overtly prefer a Black provider, the majority of women in this study strongly preferred female healthcare providers, particularly for gynecological care. In fact, 15 of 19 respondents expressed a strong preference for a female ob-gyn while almost half (9 of 19) preferred a female primary care physician. Focus group respondents expressed similar gender preferences. This finding is in keeping with a handful of studies that suggest Black women prefer female providers of any race (Casciotti

[15] Sojourner Truth posed this rhetorical question during a speech she delivered before the 1851 Women's Convention in which she questioned why Black women were not afforded the same protections and luxuries as White women. It is included here to highlight the frequent omission of gender as a salient identity for minority women, particularly in health disparities research in which race/ethnicity is foregrounded.

& Klassen, 2011; Dale, Polivka, Chaudry, & Simmonds, 2010). However, given that women comprise only 35% of practicing physicians in the United States, the supply of women physicians is unlikely to meet the demand for them (Kaiser Family Foundation, 2017).

In general, the women believed that female doctors could relate to them as a fellow woman. They suggested that they had an affinity with other women that would be impossible with male providers. They also suggested that the simple act of being listened to was one of the most important elements of the clinical encounter.

One respondent, Christina, a 43-year-old married woman who runs a home daycare business, was less circumspect in her discussion of preference:

> Uh-uh. I did one time for my ob I wanted a Black female, I did, and I wanted her because I heard so many good things about the Black female. But my husband's insurance changed so I went back to Advocate [a healthcare company]. I did want a Black ob. I don't know why, I just felt that I could relate to her more about my body. But in general, especially when I'm in pain, I don't care who it is, just let it be a doctor, I don't care, because I don't deal with pain well at all, I really don't. I don't deal with pain well at all. Only for my ob I did want a woman, but now I have a White ob doctor and I like her, too, she's pretty cool.
>
> I don't want male doctors, I'm really not that comfortable with them, so I always want a female doctor. The only male doctor I had was that Asian doctor Riley [pseudonym] when I got real sick, but I prefer, I'm comfortable with a female touching me than a male touching me. When I look for doctors, I never ever look for a male. I have one Black male doctor and that's when we had no insurance years ago and I had to go to the county. But I wasn't comfortable. And it wasn't like he did something to me, I'm just not comfortable with males, you know.

Christina's comments highlighted the influence of context on both race and gender preference. First, she noted that although she once preferred a Black female ob-gyn, her preference had softened over time. Second, her personal state of health and discomfort mitigated any potential race or gender preference. Third, depending on insurance status and physician supply, providers who fit specific demographic criteria may not be readily available.

Importantly, Christina highlighted the primacy of gender over race, at least in this context. Christina mentioned that, during a time in which she did not have a choice of provider because she was receiving care at the county hospital, she still did not want a Black male physician. In her case, having a Black doctor was much less important than having a woman. Her comments also touch on the underlying concerns at play with women and their physicians in that Christina indicates a lack of comfort with males. While she could explain her discomfort, we can speculate that, for reproductive health issues, female providers are more likely to empathize with the particular intimacies involved in such care. For Christina, this level of comfort extended to primary care as well.

Another respondent, Vanessa a 50-something divorced entrepreneur, discussed the relative comfort she felt with a female provider of any race, particularly for gynecological care:

> I like women doctors. Well, the personal stuff, definitely, I like women doctors, because they go through what you go through, and they're more sensitive, and I would think they're more knowledgeable about it just because I believe in people having experience in what they're doing, from my perspective, in that personal area of expertise. And then in other areas, I don't mind—it doesn't matter. I just want the best one I can get.

Echoing the comments of both interview and focus group respondents, Vanessa described the implicit sense of comfort she had with female ob-gyns. She also suggested that women gynecologists are more competent and knowledgeable because they have personal experience with receiving gynecological care themselves.

In sum, given that much of the disparities literature focuses on race preference without explicitly addressing the intersection of race and gender for minority women, the fact that Black women in this study preferred female providers is at once illuminating and common-sensical.

Participants believed they were more likely to receive sensitive, empathic care—gynecological care—from another woman. However, they also acknowledged that this type of care and communication is possible with male providers. The women also suggested that the context (e.g., acuity of illness, expertise of provider) matters and that relying on gender concordance alone cannot address certain challenges inherent to the healthcare encounter.

Conclusion

Women in this study provided a nuanced discussion of the characteristics they prefer and the type of interaction they want from their healthcare providers. They expressed a desire to be treated with sensitivity and compassion, which is obviously not unique to Black middle-class women. Although many women experienced positive relationships—and a sisterhood of sorts—with Black female providers, they did not necessarily seek Black female providers. This is likely due to the contextual factors (e.g., availability of female and minority physicians, insurance coverage, etc.) that constrain women's choices. Moreover, women's displeasure with the emphasis on market forces, time constraints, and the impersonal nature of American healthcare cannot be changed by having a physician of the same race or gender.

Participants also raised an important and overlooked component of the race concordance hypothesis: race preference at the healthcare site. Women intimated that their preferences do not stop at the individual provider. Rather, they suggested that the racial and socioeconomic composition of the facility, including the staff and patients, may affect their overall evaluation of the healthcare experience. In other words, Black women may use the race of provider as a proxy for the racial composition of the site, which may in turn affect whether they want a Black doctor at all. Although this finding is limited by the size of the sample, it suggests a promising new avenue for understanding the healthcare experiences of Black people and other minorities. Importantly, the women's perceptions of the healthcare facility must be understood in the overall context of how predominantly Black institutions and facilities are frequently underresourced. As such, while the participants in this study may use the race of the provider as a proxy for evaluating the quality of the healthcare site, this should not be interpreted as evidence of inherently sub-par Black facilities. Rather, the women's evaluation is likely related to the fact that the majority of minority facilities are persistently underfunded.

Furthermore, the women resoundingly demonstrated the importance of intersectionality as a framework for understanding minority women's experiences in healthcare settings. Black women have an integrated identity as both Black and female, so discussions of race that exclude gender, and vice versa, are unlikely to yield meaningful findings. Furthermore, their experiences convey both the specific connection Black women feel with each other and the universal desire to seek the best care possible, regardless of race or gender of the provider.

Yet Tammy's experience illustrates just how complex "preferences" really are. In her case, the decision to actively manage her healthcare treatment counterbalanced the profound loss of control her family endured through multiple generations. For Tammy's great-grandfather, grandmother, and others in her family, the wrong "choice"—if such a choice ever existed—could ultimately lead to loss of life. Tammy's conceptualization of "preference" suggests that contemporary decisions may be shaped by historical events and the experiences of deceased family members, in addition to individual desires.

In contrast, other women, including Shelly, Sarah, and Ellen, acknowledged that having a Black or Black female doctor alone cannot mitigate the larger problems of the healthcare system. In particular, Shelly noted that because of the emphasis on financial incentives and consumerism, having a Black female doctor could do very little to mitigate the problems that arise when providers and patients have only a 10-minute office visit in which to squeeze a complex health history and analysis of health problems. Sarah recalled her deep understanding of physicians as flawed, human beings, capable of making errors regardless of their race and gender. Finally, after suffering a life-threatening health emergency, Ellen scoffed at the idea that having a Black doctor was the most important criterion for choosing a provider. For many of these women, although race and gender are important elements of their own identities, choosing a provider based on these characteristics was far from their minds.

All told, Tammy, Ellen, Sarah, and Shelly, represent a range of Black women's opinions about the relative (un)importance of race and gender concordance. They suggest that the notion of racial and gender similarity is much more complicated than the research literature suggests. Given the stereotyping and discrimination many women experience while seeking care, some participants suggested that racial and gender similarity are the most important elements of the healthcare encounter, while others opined about what having a Black doctor signaled about the overall quality of the healthcare facility. These data indicate the range of Black women's experiences in healthcare settings and the structural barriers many of them face while trying to get the best care. Finally, although the majority of the women did not express a strong preference for a Black provider, they certainly preferred women. Black women's feelings of comfort with other women are typically absent from the conversation around health disparities. Taken together, it appears that while the Black middle-class women I interviewed for this study did not express strong preferences for Black doctors, increasing the pipeline of providers of color and female providers may indeed have a positive effect on healthcare interactions overall.

4

The Mississippi Appendectomy

Race and Reproductive Healthcare

Gender is the modality in which race is lived.
—Paul Gilroy, *Black Atlantic* (1993)

"I've been bleeding like a crazy woman for four days and either y'all gonna have to give me blood like a vampire or fix this. I don't know what the problem is." And the woman I saw, she's like, "Well, you know, you've only been bleeding quite a bit for less than two months. I'm not concerned." Tracey, a 35-year-old focus group participant[1] and an ebullient business consultant with an MBA, recalled this recent interaction with her nurse practitioner. Tracey complained of being weakened by two monthly cycles of heavy menstrual bleeding that was impossible to manage with regular sanitary products. Alarmed and fearing the embarrassment of bleeding through her clothes at work, she sought help from her provider. When Tracey described her condition, which is clearly unusual for menstruating women, her provider casually dismissed her, stating that Tracey had not been bleeding for long. The nurse brushed her off and did no further tests or examination.

However, Tracey was not deterred by the nurse's response. Her trust in healthcare providers was already tenuous, given her previous experience dealing with chronic knee pain. As a result, she was determined to advocate for more thorough attention to her symptoms.

Tracey went on to describe how she countered the provider's initial lack of concern:

> Well my answer is, "That's okay, 'cause I am [concerned]. You don't have to be concerned. You see 15 people like me. I got one like me. I'm gonna push on this. And me doing my research and having my past experience was enough for me; like, I don't let you off the hook. And I think what happens is, you know, if you still think that doctors are infallible, I get

[1] Tracey's other experiences with doctors are explored in Chapter 2.

it. They go for—the simple solution is usually the right one, but I'm not usual.

In this passage, Tracey highlights several key points that animate the remainder of this chapter. First, she notes that she simply does not accept the idea of physician's infallibility, especially given her previous experiences. Second, she emphasizes the importance of advocating for oneself in particular ways that are in keeping with the tenets of cultural health capital (e.g., conducting research about her condition and being able to convey that research in a concise, rational manner). Again, although the ability to advocate for oneself is positive, the burden of coming to the doctor with your guard up likely exacts a cumulative toll on women's health.

Last, although Tracey does not necessarily discuss how being a Black woman may have affected her care, her experience illustrates a stubbornly held belief among physicians and lay people alike. Black women are believed to be more reproductively robust than their White counterparts and therefore able to withstand more severe symptoms (Bridges, 2011; Hoberman, 2012; Roberts, 1999). Ironically, this may lead providers to dismiss Black women's complaints of pain or bleeding because they are thought to be able to tolerate more physical discomfort. That is to say, although the nurse practitioner does not explicitly say that Tracey should be more able to deal with severe bleeding than a White woman in a similar situation, her comments certainly imply that she did not take her complaint seriously. This raises the question of whether a White woman with the same symptoms would be treated in the same manner. Although it is impossible to answer that question, research on physicians' views of racial essentialism (or the idea that racial groups share a set of fixed or inherent biological and physiological characteristics[2]) suggests that a White woman complaining of severe bleeding may not have been met with such a lack of concern.

Although research on differences in treatment does not typically address how medical professionals understand and think about "race" and "racial differences," health disparities research would benefit from doing so because physician views directly affect patient care. For example, while some may interpret Tracey's experience as an indication of a rushed healthcare environment, it also illustrates

[2] As noted in Chapter 2, studies of racial differences in pain management also illustrate this point. A recent study from the University of Virginia study found that 73% of non–medically trained community members and 50% of medical students and medical residents subscribed to false beliefs about biological differences between Black and White people. Many of these ideas pertain to a differential capacity to tolerate pain and discomfort. Further analysis demonstrated that students and residents who endorsed this view were more likely to undertreat Black patients for pain in clinical simulations (Hoffman, Trawalter, Axt, & Oliver, 2016).

how physician beliefs about who is sturdy and who can tolerate pain literally determines what kind of treatment a patient receives or whether they receive treatment at all. Furthermore, in spite of the prevailing academic discourse that holds that race is a social construction, biological essentialism in medicine is by no means a thing of the past.[3]

Tracey's reproductive healthcare experiences were similar to other women in the study. Although the purpose of this work was not to explore reproductive healthcare per se, many of the participants voluntarily described their reproductive health experiences unprompted. Because I asked women open-ended questions, they were free to disclose their most salient healthcare experiences, many of which involved reproductive care. It is important to note that, although I did not specifically ask women about their reproductive health experience, so many women provided unsolicited disclosures about the topic that it suggested a larger pattern.

To better contextualize these data, this chapter begins with a discussion of the historical antecedents to contemporary reproductive healthcare specifically for Black women. It also outlines a theoretical framework from which to understand contemporary reproductive health issues—particularly in the treatment of fibroids and hysterectomy.

The chapter builds on the work of scholars of Black women's reproductive past and present, including Dorothy Roberts and Khiara M. Bridges, among others. In her seminal book, *Killing the Black Body: Race, Reproduction and the Meaning of Liberty*, Roberts (1997) notes,

> the systematic, institutionalized denial of reproductive freedom has uniquely marked Black women's history in America. Considering this history—from slave masters' economic stake in bonded women's fertility to the racist strains of early birth control policy to sterilization abuse of Black women during the 1960s and 1970s to the current campaign to inject Norplant and Depo-Provera in the arms of Black teenagers and

---

[3] There is a large body of literature on racism in medicine that analyzes the extent to which the institution of medicine and medical training reinforces racial essentialism, or the idea that members of a given group share a set of characteristics that are inherent, innate, or otherwise fixed (Morning, 2008; 2011). That is to say, scholars including Troy Duster, John Hoberman, Nancy Stepan, Ann Morning, Osagie Obasagie, and others have questioned whether medical providers, social scientists, and public health researchers have truly moved away from prewar definitions of biological race. For example, historian Nancy Stepan (1982) notes that while early understandings of race focused on physical distinctions, postwar conceptualizations emphasized the distribution of genes across population groups. As Stepan argues, although the field moved away from phenotypical variation as a marker of racial differences, the emphasis on genes preserved an ongoing belief in biological difference.

welfare mothers—paints a powerful picture of the link between race and reproductive freedom in America. (p. 4)

To flesh out these themes, the chapter uses interview and focus group data to illustrate contemporary practice patterns in which healthcare providers seemed to vacillate between practically ignoring women's healthcare concerns to recommending intensive interventions, like major surgeries, to address common gynecological problems that may be treated with less invasive procedures.[4]

Unequal Treatment: Race and Gender Differences in Medicine

The most seminal study of racial differences in treatment, the Institute of Medicine's (IOM) *Unequal Treatment* (Nelson, Stith, & Smedley, 2002), obliquely describes provider-side bias as a potential cause of differences in treatment like those described by the women in this study. Fewer epidemiological or social science studies go so far as to explore the ways in which the provider's negative perceptions of Black (and other minority) patients directly affect how they make treatment decisions. Nor do they specifically describe this antipathy as an ethical issue to be addressed by the profession as a whole (Hoberman, 2007).

The roots of this antipathy are deep in a culture of racial distinctions. Blackness has long been considered a degraded, pathological biologic entity (Bridges, 2011). It is also above all seen as something fixed. In the medical field, such perceptions hold that different races have different kinds of bodies: Blacks, Whites, Asians, and Latinos are believed to have certain immutable physical, biological, and characterological properties with corresponding behaviors and health conditions (Bridges, 2011).

Throughout the academic disciplines, theories of race as socially constructed— and not biologically determined—seem to dominate. However, a review of the literature in biomedical and life sciences suggests that, far from turning away from the racialized view of medicine that predominated in the early twentieth century (e.g., eugenics), the saliency of "biological race" in contemporary medicine and social science research methods persists (Obasogie, Harris-Wai, Darling, Keagy, & Levesque, 2014). For example, in her empirical study of how scientists think about race, sociologist Ann Morning (2011) finds: "biological

---

[4] Although I cannot evaluate the intentions of the healthcare providers, I argue that the women's *perception* of the experience is the most important interpretation of the event. Regardless of the medical facts of the specific interaction, respondents came away with their unique perspective of events that affected subsequent healthcare interactions.

interpretations of race remain powerful in scientific thinking and communications to the public, and that in contrast, the idea that race is socially constructed is not conveyed nearly as widely" (p. 6). Although much of the health disparities literature all but ignores how these beliefs may affect healthcare, it is important to consider how racial essentialism affects provider decision-making.[5]

Based on ethnographic data of a New York City public hospital's women's health clinic, anthropologist Khiara M. Bridges (2011) found that many physicians subscribe to the view of Black people's innate biological qualities, the product of what she terms "racial folklore." For example, during her work at "Alpha Hospital," Bridges noted the providers' pervasive belief that Black (and other minority) women were hyperfertile and able to endure intense discomfort during pregnancy and labor. Bridges found that providers also subscribed to a common trope about African American women in which Black mothers were considered inherently pathological, unable to care for their children, and lazy, a common finding in research on Black women's reproductive rights (Bridges, 2011; Harris-Perry, 2011; Roberts, 1997; Washington, 2006).

Bridges (2011) reports one's physician's belief that the sexual openness of many minority women, particularly Black and Latina, made it more likely that the physician would attribute any pelvic pain or gynecological discomfort to sexually transmitted disease (STD). In addition, an STD diagnosis often led to a subsequent diagnosis of pelvic inflammatory disease, which is often treated with sterilization (Roberts, 1997). This results in a kind of feedback loop in which women are diagnosed with a condition that makes a subsequent hysterectomy (or other forms of sterilization) more likely.

Ultimately, this may explain how differences in treatment lead to disparate health outcomes, including hysterectomy disparities between Black and White women.

Furthermore, historian and cultural critic John Hoberman's (2005) research on the racial attitudes of medical providers finds that providers rely on these false beliefs to determine diagnosis and treatment. He writes:

> Medical personnel who believe in Black hardiness may restrict access
> to certain kinds of surgery on the assumption that Black patients have

---

[5] The next question is whether the primacy of racial essentialism remains more salient among the scientific community because it is, in fact, more scientifically sound than the social constructionist perspective. Although this makes sense on its face, many experts believe that the empirical evidence refutes the idea of biologically grounded racial differences (G. Barbujani, 1997; Koenig, Lee, & Richardson, 2008; Marks, 1995). To the contrary, most of the evidence points to incredible genetic similarity across all human beings regardless of outward appearance (Barbujani, Magagni, Minch, & Cavalli-Sforza, 1997; Lewontin, 1972).

a less urgent need for such procedures. Conversely, the same belief in
Black hardiness may account for the disproportionate frequency with
Black patients are subjected to more radical and damaging surgeries
than whites: hysterectomies, lower-limb amputations, and bilateral
orchidectomies (castration), since medical personnel may assume they
are better able to tolerate such trauma. (p. 96)

Hoberman's (2007) analysis of such treatment incorporates the historical legacy
of early racialized thinking that "distinguishes between civilized and primitive
peoples" (p. 94).

Hoberman also asserts that although the medical establishment no longer
overtly endorses this racial logic, notions of Black hardiness are adapted to modern circumstances and endure in medical schools, hospitals, and medical care
in general (Hoberman, 2005; 2012). Moreover, although Hoberman (2007)
makes a compelling argument for the explicit role of physician racism in causing health disparities, he also notes the enormous lengths the medical establishment has gone to avoid this characterization. This may explain why there is
great discomfort among scholars and lay people alike in considering how both
implicit and explicit bias may directly impact patient care. But Hoberman cor-
rectly points out that there is no reason to assume that physicians are immune to
stereotyping or racism. They are no more likely than others to escape the biases
and prejudices that are rampant in the social milieu in which we live, including
in medical schools and medical settings. In fact, one might argue that persistence of racial essentialism may lead physicians to even more calcified beliefs
about innate biological differences between racial groups. As a result, he argues
that ideas of racial hardiness linger in the medical establishment's beliefs about
Black women. According to Hoberman, physicians believe that Black women,
and other ethno-racial minorities, have a "primitive pelvis," corresponding to
their primitive nature, which renders them reproductively healthy. The idea of
the primitive pelvis is then tacitly used both as a justification for lack of treatment *and* more radical or invasive surgeries (Hoberman, 2005).

Hoberman (2012) and Bridges (2011) carefully situate their critiques
of the medical profession in the larger context of stereotyping and historic
medico-social abuses of the Black population. For example, even during the
early twentieth century, eugenicists relied on stereotypes of Black women as
sexually indiscriminate bad mothers who gave birth to biologically defective
children to arrive at a biological explanation of Black pathology (Washington,
2006). Washington (2006) writes that, according to eugenicists, "the sexual
irrepressibility and the bad mothering were biologically located in the heredi-
tary apparatus . . . thus eugenics undergirded medicosocial movements that
placed the sexual behavior and reproduction of Blacks under strict scrutiny and

disproportionately forced them into sterility, both temporary and permanent" (p. 192).

Washington (2006) goes on to document the extensive use of forced and coerced hysterectomy. She tells the story of the famed activist Fannie Lou Hamer, who was propelled into political action after a doctor performed a hysterectomy on her without her consent during a 1961 surgery to remove a uterine fibroid. According to Washington, rendering a southern Black woman infertile without her knowledge was so common in the 1960s that the procedure came to be known as a "Mississippi appendectomy." However, the South was not the only region to support involuntary hysterectomies because they were also commonly practiced throughout the country for multiple reasons, including allowing medical residents to "practice" their surgical skills and limiting reproduction among poor women on welfare (Washington, 2006).

Given this history, and because Black people and other minorities are often viewed as "other," providers may come to view their patients as fundamentally different from themselves. Moreover, although the health disparities and social science literature is largely silent about how class moderates the effect of race on physician's perception of patients, there is little reason to believe that essentialist views would differ by the class standing of the patient. If "race" is thought to be a fixed biological entity, the patient's profession, education, or income would do little to mitigate the provider's preconceived ideas about Black women.

"Nurse Ratchet and the Typical Black Woman"

> People make attributions about you. They decide who you are.
> —Jennifer, 38, police detective

Women in general, and Black women in particular, have always been bound by societal expectations about their bodies and sexuality. Particularly with regard to sexual expression and reproductive freedom, women are judged, cajoled, or otherwise controlled by the sexual mores of the dominant society (Collins, 2000). However, as noted earlier, Black women have had to navigate a particularly pernicious form of raced and gendered reproductive regulation. The scholarly attention to these forms of discrimination has focused primarily on poor Black women, but, as evidenced by the data that follow, Black middle-class women are also affected by "misogynoir."[6] Moreover, although the ways in which stereotyping, bias, and discrimination manifest may vary (e.g., from poor interpersonal

---

[6] The term "misogynoir," first coined by gender studies scholar Moya Bailey (2010; 2016), refers to anti-Black and misogynistic racism directed at Black women.

treatment from a triage nurse to being advised to have a hysterectomy at 27 years old), these data suggest an ongoing pattern in line with past regimes of reproductive control.

Jennifer, a 38-year-old Chicago police detective who I interviewed in a Southside coffee shop, had a casual, easy demeanor that seemed to run counter to being a hardscrabble cop. Although she was tall and athletic, her face still looked like a teenager's. Throughout the interview she described her experience with healthcare providers, which ranged from generally positive to nondescript. As a result of a negative experience with her father's foreign-born physician, she indicated her only preference was for American providers with whom she felt she could communicate more easily. Because she was young and healthy, her healthcare experiences were relatively straightforward, and, throughout the interview, she insisted that employer-sponsored health insurance, not her race or gender, was the most important determinant of receiving unbiased high-quality healthcare.

However, as we discussed the healthcare system in general, she disclosed two deeply personal and painful events of her early adulthood. When she was 18 years old, she became pregnant by her steady boyfriend and reluctantly decided to have an abortion. Only 1 month after the abortion, she was sexually assaulted on her way to school. She reflected,

> Years ago when I was 18, I had gotten pregnant. And I had an abortion. . . . And about a month later on my way to school I had gotten attacked. So I was assaulted . . . [she then laughed nervously] I'm okay. I'm okay.
>
> . . . I had to go to the hospital. And there were two white nurses.
>
> But anyway. . . . At the hospital, they were very nice to me. You know I was not hysterical. I told them what they wanted to know, and they put me down on the table. And when she—they were very nice and compassionate about what happened. And when they went to go stick the speculum inside of me, it was very, very painful. And they had a hard time getting it in . . . .she had a hard time getting in, and I was jerking around 'cause it was so painful.

Although Jennifer remained composed as she recounted her story, she had undoubtedly endured two extremely traumatic events, a rape and an abortion both within a month's time and at only 18 years of age. Even the subsequent healthcare encounter was traumatic and physically painful. In telling the story, Jennifer emphasized that the encounter went well at first, which she suggested was due to her controlled demeanor and absence of hysteria. Maintaining steely rationality in the face of intense emotions is a trait often associated with the

Strong Black Woman trope discussed in Chapter 1. The fact that she felt she needed to be calm also hints at how hard it was for her to let her guard down and trust the people who were putatively there to help her. Also, although Jennifer was just emerging into womanhood, she seemed to have already internalized the importance of presenting herself in a composed rational manner even in the most vulnerable situations. Last, she emphasized her sexual piety when she noted that she had only had one sexual partner at the time of the incident.

Jennifer went on to describe how the provider's attitude toward her changed as the exam progressed,

> She was like, "Oh, you have something." She just assumed I had something . . . "Oh, you have an infection. It looks—from the smell of it, it looks like gonorrhea." And her whole attitude changed, like she didn't care that this happened to me. Like I probably deserved it. You know she was just very rude. One of them stayed nice. There were two women doctors as well. The one of them stayed very nice. Real quiet lady, very nice. She remained compassionate.
>
> The other one just completely—she was just like, "Well we can't do this, and this smells down there. And it sounds like—it looks like you have gonorrhea or something. So we're gonna have to take the blood test." And she kinda like threw it [the speculum] down. "And we're not gonna be able to go through with the [exam]" 'cause they were trying to do the rape kit. . . . She just completely flipped out and changed on me. And I was embarrassed—and humiliated.

Although Jennifer seemed appreciative of the doctor who maintained a sense of decency and compassion, the other provider humiliated her. She explained further,

> [At first] she was compassionate toward me. "Oh, poor little thing. You're a little school-aged girl going to school and somebody raped you." But now that you [seem to have an STD], oh, that's not what happened. [Then they asked Jennifer if she had had an STD previously]— I was like, "No." And I said this to them. "'Has anything happened?" I said, "Well, I did have an abortion a month ago." That's when her attitude changed.
>
> I became another type of a person, like some—I don't know what she thought I was—her whole idea of me just completely changed for the worst. And she walked out. And then she told me—she automatically put down—saying that I had it [*gonorrhea*]. I didn't have that. . . .

'Cause like people make attributions about you. They decide who
you are based on things.

Jennifer's interpretation of these events suggests that she was aware of the
stereotypes Black women face particularly with regard to their alleged sexual
lasciviousness. As described in Chapter 1, the Jezebel stereotype is among
the most persistently negative characterizations of Black women. Importantly,
Black women's supposed hypersexuality and predatory tendencies, which the
Jezebel stereotype represents, were often used to justify their sexual victimization. Furthermore, Jennifer acknowledges that, for her providers, her previous
sexual activity and possible STD transformed her from a blameless rape victim
into a just another young Black woman of ill repute, akin to a "working girl" (or
prostitute).

Add an abortion to the mix and the situation became even more highly
charged. In fact, Jennifer believed her provider's contempt for her stemmed from
her disdain for women who have abortions. In fact, Jennifer was very conflicted
over her decision to have the abortion at all:

> I didn't want to have [the abortion]. I felt bad. But then I was scared. I'm
> like, I was young. And it was a hard decision, but [the doctor]—in her
> mind, she was like, "Oh, she's just a working little girl. She's out there
> having sex, getting pregnant, get an abortion. Now she got raped, she
> can deal with that. That ain't nothing." That's how her attitude became
> at that point. And then she gave me pills to take as though I had [a sexu-
> ally transmitted disease].

She also reflected on her experience based on her current position as a detective:

> And I see that at my job all the time with girls, too. So I kinda—it reg-
> isters. How they walk in, we have a lot of rape victims. And they walk
> in looking a certain way, oh well. Oh, they got raped. Well they can
> handle it.

One could argue that Jennifer was treated in such a manner because the provider had moral objections to the abortion, which is certainly possible. However,
because the sexual stereotypes of Black women are so pervasive, it is difficult
to tease out exactly what displeased the provider. It could have been the com-
pounding effect of the abortion, the presumed STD, and Jennifer's own sense of
shame about the abortion. Based on Jennifer's status as a young Black woman,
the provider may have perceived her as a sexually available and irresponsible
woman who casually resorted to abortion. The fact that Jennifer had just been

sexually assaulted and the provider was there to provide care and collect possible evidence seemed far from her mind. Finally, the provider was quick to diagnose her with an STD without the proper examination or lab testing. The potentially stigmatizing STD diagnosis led Jennifer to question herself:

> For a minute I thought I did have it. I was thinking, *Do I have it?*
>
> ... I went back to the hospital for a check-up because I was taking the pills. . . . And then I asked them, did I have any symptoms of anything that went away. And they told me some type of bacteria infection or something that I had. So it wasn't gonorrhea. But that's what she diagnosed me with.

Although it is unclear if Jennifer had an STD, she certainly interpreted the provider's diagnosis and other actions as a rejection of who she was, generally, and her decision to have an abortion, specifically. Given the complexity of the situation, it is difficult to know exactly how the provider's personal beliefs about abortion were also shaped by negative characterizations of Black women in general.[7] However, regardless of the provider's perspective, the bottom line is that Jennifer was an 18-year-old sexual assault survivor and her previous health history, including the abortion and the STD, should have been irrelevant.

Another focus group participant named Eve, a woman in her 50s, described a similar judgment of her character during an encounter she had during her first pregnancy. She described her physical appearance at the time of the incident, emphasizing her Afro- centric hairstyle and the absence of her wedding ring, which she was not wearing because her hand was swollen as a result of her pregnancy. Eve described the encounter:

> I must have had Nurse Ratchet because she treated me like I was an unwed mother. And I was so upset because I had a top doctor on Michigan Avenue. I was paid up because they make sure you pay up before you deliver back in those days. And this woman treated me so bad.
>
> I was just hurt. When my husband came in and, you know, at this time I'm like in tears. I'm upset. I'm like, "She's acting like, you know, I don't have any money, treating me like, you know, I was just a typical Black, unwed, young woman." And I was so hurt by that experience, you know.

---

[7] As is the case with all the experiences reported by the respondents, I do not have access to the physician's point of view of the incidents reported in the study. As such, I am implicitly privileging the perspective of the women in the study.

I have to say one of the most negative things because, you know, I went to 29 [before having her first child]; I'm married. I'm doing all the right—I mean I've done all the right things. I had a college degree, you know paid for the Dr. So-and-So on Michigan Avenue. And this woman treated me so bad, my husband had to finally come in and he, you know, he set it straight. Then the healthcare changed 100 percent when she knew that I had someone with me.

Eve spoke of the incident, which occurred about 25 years earlier, with a combination of humor, anguish, and disgust. She described her efforts to do the right things, to get married, and complete her college degree. She alluded to stereotypes of uncontrolled, nonmarital fertility (i.e., the Jezebel) among young Black women as well as her efforts to resist those characterizations. However, she also suggests an internalization of the idea that she had to be married, have a college degree, and a husband to be considered worthy of motherhood or to seek healthcare without judgment. She expressed great frustration with the fact that, although she tried to do "all the right things," which included a considerable amount of work to complete her degree and enter into a stable marital relationship, she was still being judged based on long-standing stereotypes of Black women. She also suggested that her treatment, which improved after her husband arrived on the scene, was affected by the nurse's hetero-normative, sexist assumption that men must "vouch" for women's character, particularly Black women. Eve felt strongly that the nurse's initial perception of her was based on racist, sexist, and heterosexist stereotypes and biases.

Finally, although the incidents Eve and Jennifer described took place several years ago, their impact lingered well into the present. Both women seemed deeply affected by the way they were treated. Although these data do not allow me to determine how their reproductive healthcare experiences affected their subsequent engagement with providers, it is possible that these foundational experiences may have led to a sense of distrust or reticence to engage. As a result, early negative experiences may ripple into the women's future, thereby acting as an additional social determinant of health.

The Mississippi Appendectomy: Black Women, Fibroids and Hysterectomy

> They did the ultrasound and she [the provider] was like, "We need to do a hysterectomy." And I was just like, "I'm 27 years old, don't have any kids. What are we talking about?"
>
> —Monica, focus group participant

Similar to Jennifer and Eve, several of the women I encountered during the in-depth interviews and focus groups expressed their dismay with reproductive healthcare, specifically with regard to uterine fibroids and hysterectomy. Seven interview respondents and two focus group respondents reported that they were advised to have hysterectomies at relatively young ages and for a variety of underlying conditions.

Certainly, there are medical indications for having the procedure, but, given the historic and contemporary backdrop of forced sterilization, the fact that nine relatively young (<45) healthy women from different walks of life had similar experiences piqued my curiosity. The commonality between poor Black and middle-class Black women suggests that a system of raced and gendered discrimination, both on the individual and institutional levels, may have impacted how they were treated.

Moreover, although it is clear that reproductive healthcare is a contentious, vulnerable, and anxiety-provoking experience for many women, Black women described the additional burden of being Black particularly with regard to treatment for uterine fibroid tumors (a common condition among Black women). Women in the study specifically felt that physicians disproportionately recommended hysterectomies as a first-line treatment for fibroid tumors even when less invasive surgical options were available.

As background to the data presented here, it is important to describe just how common uterine fibroids and hysterectomies are in Black women. According to a 2017 study, up to 80% of Black women will have fibroids by menopause while 70% of White women are likely to have them by the same age (Eltoukhi, Modi, Weston, Armstrong, & Stewart, 2014; Hellwege et al., 2017). In addition, fibroids affect African American women differently through the life course; Black women are more likely to have tumors, to have them at a younger age, and to have continued growth of their tumors longer than their White counterparts (Eltoukhi et al., 2014). Fibroids are the leading cause of hysterectomy in the United States, accounting for between 33% and 40% of all hysterectomies performed (Wechter, Stewart, Myers, Kho, & Wu, 2011). Although less invasive interventions such as uterine fibroid embolization (UFE) and magnetic resonance–guided focused-ultrasound surgery exist, these procedures are used much less often than hysterectomy. Finally, although uterine fibroids disproportionately affect Black women, in some cases significantly curtailing quality of life, federal research on the condition is not commensurate with its prevalence in the US population.

In addition to suffering from fibroids at a greater rate than their White counterparts, Black women were 3.5 times more likely to be hospitalized for fibroids compared to their White counterparts; 2.4 times more likely to have a hysterectomy than White women; and, more generally, Black women were hospitalized at a greater rate for fibroid surgery, including both hysterectomy and myomectomy (where the uterus is left intact) (Eltoukhi et al., 2014; Wechter et al., 2011). Current studies cite the same rates as just presented, using the same sources, which is symptomatic of research disparities in uterine fibroids: According to a 2010 review, 75% of fibroid studies did not report race and, of the 25% that did, only 15% of those study participants were Black women (Eltoukhi et al., 2014; Taran, Brown, & Stewart, 2010). Black women between 40 and 44 years of age have a hysterectomy rate of 16.8 per 1,000 compared to 10.8 for White women. The overall estimated hysterectomy rate for Black women was 6.2 per 1,000 compared to 5.3 per 1,000 for White women, which was not statistically significant. Interestingly, however, the higher hysterectomy rates for Black women of childbearing age (35–44 years) were statistically significant (CDC, MMWR, 2002). Overall, although it is difficult to disentangle the underlying prevalence of fibroids among Black women from their higher rates of hysterectomy, these data suggest that Black women still suffer a disproportionate burden of in-patient hospitalization and invasive surgery compared to their White counterparts (Eltoukhi et al., 2014).

Although Black women have a much higher rate of uterine fibroids than White women, the women I spoke to had varying opinions about the appropriate treatment for them. Some women felt their hysterectomies were medically necessary while others saw the procedure as a way to control Black women's reproduction. What their experiences had in common, however, was that although the specific circumstances differed, each reported that physicians were quick to recommend removal of the uterus—regardless of the severity of the condition. Some women had asymptomatic pelvic conditions while others suffered from heavy bleeding that severely curtailed their quality of life. In spite of the differences in their symptoms, each felt that physicians quickly defaulted to recommending an extreme surgical intervention.

Many women discussed the lack of empathy with which they were treated, including in situations in which the provider was also Black. For example, Monica, a focus group respondent in her 40s, recalled hearing the diagnosis from of a Black female gynecologist:

> I was 27 years old. I was diagnosed—I had basically a cyst on my ovaries and I—I was going to a Black gynecologist all of my adult life. They did the ultrasound and everything and she was more like, "We need to do a hysterectomy." And I was just like, "I'm 27 years old, don't have any kids. What are we talking about?"
>
> And she had no sympathy. She was just really cold and just everything. And I actually talked to my mother and she was like, "Get a second opinion, definitely." And I went to a White doctor and actually got

a better response. And it was like, "There is no need for that. You need to just, you know, try to remove just the cyst." And he was willing to do the operation himself. He was chief oncologist at Northwestern. So it was pretty interesting. I try to stay away from Black doctors.

Monica's experience is curious in that removing a woman's *uterus* does not seem to be an appropriate treatment for an *ovarian* cyst. Although it is impossible to interpret the physician's motivation, recommending a hysterectomy to a 27-year-old childless woman seems unreasonable. Moreover, having a Black gynecologist did not protect Monica from such casual, permanent, and drastic treatment for one ovarian cyst. Rather, the physician's recommendation was in line with the pervasive practice of recommending that Black women undergo hysterectomy even for relatively minor conditions. Monica also suggested that, in spite of the fact that her doctor was also a Black woman, she had internalized the stereotypes of Black women, which then led her to advise such intensive intervention.

As was the case with other respondents, it is impossible to intuit the provider's thought process or to clarify the clinical circumstances that precipitated the hysterectomy recommendation. However, given the pervasiveness of recommending hysterectomies to Black women, it is possible that the provider thought the surgery was the simplest and best treatment option. The physician's assessment of the patient and her condition may have been influenced by prevailing notions about young Black women, whether she herself was a Black woman or not. Moreover, given the prevailing notions of racial essentialism and Black hardiness, perhaps the physician's medical school training suggested this was the most appropriate course of treatment. However, it seems almost incredible to think of recommending that a 27-year-old White childless woman have a hysterectomy for a single ovarian cyst. However, we know that Black women are still more likely than White women to be pressured or misled into having a hysterectomy, often as a treatment for fibroids or endometriosis, which can be treated with much more conservative surgeries and medications (Washington, 2006).

Bobbi, the 46-year-old finance executive introduced in Chapter 3, had a similar experience with her Black female ob-gyn when she was diagnosed with one fibroid tumor:

So I make an appointment, go see her. [The doctor says] "you need a hysterectomy." Yeah. "You need a hysterectomy," and I'm just in shock when somebody says that. Do you know what her response to me was? "Are you gonna cry or something?"

I walked out of her office. I was just upset. I was pissed, and I walked back downtown, 'cause I just lost it.

So I start calling my friends who had any sort of fibroids or anything, and then that's how I got to Dr. K. And so I call his office and we have a consultation, and he's, like, "I'll take you on as a patient." He says, "No, you do not need to have a hysterectomy for one fibroid. No, no you don't."

Both women had to seek a second opinion and become advocates for their health to avoid their original health provider's recommendation. However, both Bobbi and Monica were middle-class women with the financial and informational resources to seek a second opinion. Both women sought counsel from other women in their social networks who suggested they get a second opinion. Although the reproductive regime of using hysterectomies to treat relatively minor conditions seems to cut across race, Black middle-class women have more resources to avoid the fates of many poor Black women who may not have the information or the money to seek care elsewhere.

Another respondent, Sarah, the 40-year-old network manager for an insurance company described in Chapter 3, had been diagnosed with fibroids in her 20s. At age 40, Sarah was told that she had a "grossly enlarged" uterus and that hysterectomy was her best option for permanent relief. Like Bobbi and Monica, Sarah had access to information, and her career in the health insurance industry meant she was very comfortable maneuvering through the system. She researched alternatives to hysterectomy like UFE, and, as a result, she resisted the idea that she *had* to have a hysterectomy. Sarah recounted her experience with her gynecologist:

And these last couple of years I've had a couple of issues with fibroids. . . . And it's funny because I went to my gyny and I love her as well, I think she's really good, but she was quick to like "Let's do the hysterectomy . . . we just need to get rid of it, be done with it, but unfortunately your uterus is so large that we're going to have to actually cut."

Because I was just like, "I can't do that. I can't take two to three months off work. I'm a single parent. I can't do that. How large is it?"

"Oh, you're about six months pregnant large." And I'm like, "Are you kidding me!" So I actually found [a different doctor]. Dr. V. Because she was like, "Let's just get rid of it, let's cut it out and get rid of it." But I'm not doing that.

Definitely, I know that that would have offered me a lot of relief. I felt like it would have also created some other problems like premature menopause and all of that kind of stuff. So looking at it from that perspective, and then I'm a single parent, my income is it, that's a long time, and in this economy.

Although Sarah had a long-term positive relationship with her physician, the physician was quick to suggest a major surgery and casually described it as "getting rid of it," referring to Sarah's uterus. Recall Hoberman's (2005) critique of the medical establishment's belief in racial essentialism in which he notes, "Black hardiness may account for the disproportionate frequency with Black patients are subjected to more radical and damaging surgeries than whites [including] hysterectomies" (p. 96). The physician's use of phrases like "cut it out" and "get rid of it" suggest a profound lack of empathy for her patients.

Similar to the other women in this study, Sarah was in a position to use her access to information and ability to sift through the healthcare system to find another doctor.

However, it is important to note that although she is ostensibly middle class, Sarah is a single parent supporting a teenage son on her single income. In addition to her concerns about the side effects of the hysterectomy, she feared having such an invasive surgery that may have required her to stop working to recover. For many members of the middle class, particularly Black women who tend to make less money than their White or male counterparts (Blau, 2016; Deaton, 2002; Cooper et al., 2001), medical decisions are intertwined with financial realities.

Furthermore, Sarah's experience raises an important question about the medical management of fibroids and the use of hysterectomy as treatment. First, Sarah was diagnosed many years earlier and was told to adopt a "watchful waiting" approach. However, once the symptoms became unbearable, Sarah's physician noted that, because her uterus was so distorted from the fibroids, the only long-term solution was to "cut it out and get rid of it." This treatment strategy begs the question: why do physicians advise patients to wait until their tumors are so large that the most viable option is hysterectomy? And, if Sarah, Bobbi, and Monica are any indication, providers are not particularly gentle or empathic as they deliver healthcare advice that will fundamentally alter a woman's life.

Other focus group participants were unequivocal in their view that hysterectomies are overused among Black women:

> I mean, I felt that my hysterectomy could have been Michigan Avenue paying for the rent because I wasn't bleeding heavy. I just had a huge tumor and I took some medicine. And, if I had known that there were other alternatives, I would have done the alternatives.
>
> So sometimes I think things are financial for business. I used to think there must be a big utero pile there because everyone that I knew was getting [*hysterectomies*]—or they were using it for penile implants or using it for something.

Cause everybody I know—everybody was getting a hysterectomy. Like what is this, the going thing to be 40 or 45 and 48 and you're getting a hysterectomy? You know? But it was a real phase.

Although the women described the prevalence of hysterectomies among their friends in a tongue-in-cheek manner, they clearly heard the recommendation for surgery presented in a cavalier manner, as if the doctors all held the view that Black women were hardy enough to endure the physical procedure, the physical and emotional recovery, and the potential side effects. Brenda also discussed wanting to learn more about different treatment options, a theme that was expressed by all of the women with whom I spoke.

Finally, they were not shy in pointing out the financial incentives that are built into the healthcare system, jokingly noting that their surgeries paid the rent on the doctor's office in expensive downtown Chicago.

Unlike many of the women in this study who characterized their healthcare experiences as generally positive, Bella,[8] a 55-year-old woman, had a far less rosy view. When I asked her whether she thought being a Black woman affected her experiences with doctors she said,

> First of all, there's just no—the respect is not there. There's no respect like there should be for a person, period . . . that's the main thing, respect. They expect us to just take anything. They'll give you anything and expect you to take it—the medication. They'll say, "This is for this," and they don't expect to answer too many questions—or to ask too many questions . . . a lot of them are not personable, as they should be—you're talking about your life, and a doctor is treating you like it's nothing, like you're a number instead of a person. We understand in the world we are numbers, but to your doctor, you expect to be a person.

Bella was deeply frustrated by the lack of respect she felt was directly related to being a Black woman. Bella's comments illustrate the tenets of cultural health capital in that she tried to counter the lack of respect by,

> Reading more, asking more questions, get a much better understanding of what was going on, you know, and I would wanna know exactly what you're going to do, okay? But you know what, that doesn't always work.

[8] Bella's experience of sexual mistreatment at the hands of a White physician in the segregated South was discussed in Chapter 2.

However, although Bella tried to be an informed healthcare consumer, she still regretted having a hysterectomy,

> I had a hysterectomy, which I probably didn't have to have, because I had endometriosis—but I probably could've got around it. Knowing that, with—dealing with the holistic doctor, he said there was a way around it; I didn't have to have that.
>
> I was in my 30s—yeah. In fact, I was reading something about that— it's like they wanna give us hysterectomies. They're trying to stop the population from growing, aren't they? So they may tell a young girl— even younger than I was—that you have to have a hysterectomy. And why they would do me like that, I don't know, because I only had two daughters.

Bella's endometriosis was severe, and she admitted that because of the pain she was almost willing to do anything to stop it. But she was frustrated that hysterectomy was the only treatment option offered to her. It is possible that the surgery was, in fact, the best intervention, but for Bella, recommending a hysterectomy to a woman in her 30s harkened back to the Mississippi Appendectomy or the state-sponsored forced sterilizations that were common in the South. Bella had grown up in Mississippi under the racial strictures of Jim Crow. As a result, the idea of the Mississippi Appendectomy was not far-fetched. She also felt that suggesting a hysterectomy to a woman in her 30s who only had two children was drastic. Although Bella did not necessarily want more children, she wistfully stated that she had passing thoughts of trying for a boy until that was obviously no longer an option.

Bella's account is surely not isolated or insignificant. She described how the hysterectomy thrust her into early menopause, and she had many medical and emotional complications as a result. As discussed in Chapter 2, she had already endured years of trauma at the hands of the medical establishment—including being repeatedly sexually molested by a White male family practitioner—only to have her fertility taken away to address a gynecological problem for which there may have been less invasive treatment options.

Conclusion

Taken together, the women's experiences point to the sometimes subtle and sometimes explicit ways that enduring stereotypes and negative judgments about Black women—bolstered by a long history of discrimination—permeate reproductive healthcare. Their experiences support earlier research that found

Black women may experience differences in treatment—affecting tests, diagnoses, and recommended procedures—which may be a result of racial essentialism in the medical profession and long-standing negative perceptions about Black women (Bridges, 2011; Hoberman, 2005).

For example, Tracey's comments, in which she describes her provider's nonchalance regarding heavy bleeding caused by fibroids, support Hoberman's (2005) claim that Black women are treated as if they possess a certain gynecological hardiness. Although she complained of heavy bleeding, she did not perceive her provider to be responsive. Her provider's lack of concern and Hoberman's thesis together suggest that symptoms of gynecological problems in Black women may just be considered par for the course.

In Jennifer's case, her experience with a seemingly judgmental doctor following a sexual assault left her full of self-doubt and perhaps additionally traumatized. Instead of encountering a supportive female healthcare provider, she was humiliated. Jennifer's experience of feeling judged highlights the potential mechanisms through which stereotyping may have a profound effect on the patient–provider relationship, health outcomes, and, ultimately, health disparities. Similar to many other women in the study, Jennifer's past experience may reverberate into the present, suggesting that the social determinants of health occur across different time periods. In other words, past negative experiences likely affect present and future healthcare engagement.

Furthermore, given that Black women bear a disproportionate burden of uterine fibroids, it may seem unremarkable that 9 of 30 study participants were advised to have the surgery at relatively young ages. However, the commonality of the surgery in this small sample raises many questions. For example, why was a woman in her prime reproductive age advised to have a hysterectomy without regard for maintaining her fertility? Why would the removal of the uterus be the first intervention for fibroids instead of a less intensive surgery like UFE?

Although the data presented throughout privilege the perspective of women patients, and without access to the provider's rationale, it is difficult to know why certain decisions were made or treatment recommendations were handed down. However, given what we do know about the persistence of racial essentialism in medicine, the disproportionate rates of hysterectomy among Black women, and the history of coerced hysterectomies at the hands of the state, I argue that the women's stories suggest a persistent pattern in the reproductive regulation of Black women. These data suggest there is certainly more to learn about how medical training and both explicit and implicit bias affects clinical decision-making and what, if anything, we can do to improve it.

5

Conclusion

Not everything that is faced can be changed, but nothing can be changed until it is faced.

—James Baldwin

If Black women were free, it would mean that everyone else would have to be free since our freedom would necessitate the destruction of all the systems of oppression.

—Combahee River Collective (1995)

Throughout this book, I have argued that Black middle-class women's struggle to get the best treatment in the American healthcare system is invisible. Although the women in this study worked for a living and had health insurance and decent educations, they continued to feel the sting of racial and gender discrimination. However, in spite of their similarities with other poor women of color, middle-class Black women are not typically thought of as a vulnerable social group, which obscures their unique challenges. A main thrust of this book is to raise the profile of Black women who are not poor but face ongoing discrimination—in healthcare settings and beyond.

Furthermore, the empirical evidence presented here paints a subtle and troubling picture of how differences in treatment persist across socioeconomic status and the ways Black middle-class women try, often unsuccessfully, to use their social and cultural health capital resources to get the best care possible. The findings also point to much larger issues that must be addressed if we are to ever truly grapple with discrimination and inequity. First, the framing of health disparities research and intervention is far too narrow to address the underlying causes and consequences of differences in treatment. To effectively deal with the problem, we must reckon with the broader context of structural discrimination, which precedes and compounds healthcare inequities. As physician scholar Jonathon Metzl (2010) has argued, situating the problem of healthcare disparities solely at the nexus of the patient and provider makes it difficult to address the contextual factors that undoubtedly affect these individuals well before they enter the exam room. Interventions that stop at pairing a Black provider with a Black patient as a corrective for widespread systematic discrimination are simply too limited to address pervasive and cumulative barriers to respectful, high-quality medical care.

Second, although it may be more comfortable to suggest that inequities are the result of implicit bias, we must acknowledge the very real phenomenon of explicit bias, which may take forms ranging from overt racial antipathy to the dismissal of patient's requests for pain medication. Furthermore, cultural critic and historian John Hoberman (2012) has argued that the American medical establishment has long relied on racial descriptions to explain socially patterned differences in human health. He notes that American medicine "devised racial interpretations that have been applied to every organ system of the human body" (Hoberman, 2012, p. 2). As such, it is a mistake to conclude that racial differences in healthcare treatment are necessarily accidental or subconscious. Rather, they are more likely a natural outgrowth of American medical training and practice.

Moreover, the biases and overtly discriminatory views that are built into healthcare practice are scarcely acknowledged by medical providers as a whole,[1] thereby making it very difficult to address them.

We must also recognize that both implicit and explicit bias and discriminatory treatment are not the exclusive provenance of medical students, physicians, or healthcare institutions. Rather, they are part and parcel of a society that has not addressed its "original sins" and deepest divisions.[2] By framing the debate around health disparities as a benign process through which Black women (and others) receive less than the standard of care in medical settings, we avoid the dirty little secret about the American healthcare system and the United States more generally. Pervasive stereotyping, and the particularly pernicious antipathy toward Black women, affects clinical decision-making and is literally bad for Black women's health. Furthermore, being middle class or being able to engage healthcare providers rationally and efficiently cannot mitigate profoundly sexist and anti-Black biases. It must also be noted that although increasing the proportion of Black and female healthcare providers is important, the problem is much bigger than pairing Black female patients with Black female providers. We are well past the point of recommending superficial fixes to the healthcare system. We must move into a phase of profound reckoning with the underlying challenges that characterize the US healthcare system.

[1] Although I argue that the medical establishment has not acknowledged the discriminatory assumptions built into medical training and practice, many physicians are making a concerted effort to raise the issue within the medical profession (Acosta & Ackerman-Barger, 2017).

[2] To be clear, I am not arguing that these divisions are simply interpersonal. Rather, racial, sex, and economic exploitation in the United States represents a system of power that leads to disparate health, economic, and social outcomes.

Health-Related Stereotype Threat and the Healthcare Encounter

Although many of the women I interviewed described positive experiences with healthcare providers regardless of whether women were lower middle- or upper middle-class, they also expressed the need to steel themselves against stereotyping, bias, and discrimination. The fact that they anticipate stereotyping in healthcare settings (i.e., health-related stereotype threat) and try to adjust their behavior to mitigate it, is largely invisible to most people, including health disparities researchers. The behavioral adjustments the women made, from emphasizing their intelligence to conducting research prior to the encounter, are also imperceptible. But their efforts to manage their persona and, in turn, the encounter may have far-reaching consequences for their relationship with the provider and their own health.

In spite of the challenges women faced in healthcare settings, some had excellent relationships with their providers, which they credited with saving their lives. In contrast to the research suggesting that having a Black provider improves the patient–provider relationship, which in turn improves health outcomes, many of the positive relationships were not in race concordant pairs. That is to say, many of their most positive experiences were with White or non-Black providers.

However, women pointed to the overwhelming influence of financial incentives as one of the most problematic parts of the healthcare system, one that cannot be fixed simply by having a Black doctor. Some women happened upon a doctor who listened and took their concerns seriously, which ultimately seemed to be the most important element of the healthcare encounter. Other women were not so fortunate and frequently encountered callous or superficial treatment. In the case of Tracey, who could have lost her leg to tumors in her knee, or Jennifer, who was raped and treated as though it was her fault because she was already sexually active, the cavalier treatment had far-reaching implications on the way they perceived doctors and the healthcare system writ large.

In spite of the struggles these women reported, many researchers overlook the ways that race and gender discrimination continue to affect minority women who are not poor. Furthermore, focusing exclusively on the relationships among race, poverty, and health forecloses the opportunity to analyze how discrimination affects the health of racial and ethnic minorities across class status.

Adapting to Health-Related Stereotype Threat

This study's findings, gleaned from the experiences of Black middle-class women themselves, suggest an interpretation that departs from the dominant paradigm on discrimination in healthcare. First, they point to prevailing negative stereotypes about Black women that follow them into the doctor's visit despite their class or educational status. Given that women anticipated stereotyping and bias, they tried to emphasize certain elements of their persona particularly vis-à-vis their cultural health capital. In other words, to be visible to their providers, they tried to leverage certain skills that are valued in the contemporary healthcare space, such as the ability to convey health information in a rational and efficient manner or take an instrumental approach to one's body, among others. But simply being able to do your research before you arrive at the doctor and then communicate it efficiently does not necessarily ensure you get the best care. In fact, the women in the study pointed to the burden of always feeling like they had to jockey for position at the doctor's office. As much as women in this study discussed the strategies they used to try to mitigate stereotypes and bias, there is often very little that can be done to change the provider's preconceived ideas about certain patients.

The findings also highlight Black women's hidden daily labor, the cumulative burden of which may explain why Black women have poorer health outcomes compared to White women. Furthermore, although feeling as though you must advocate for yourself at all times is exhausting, the women's efforts should also be understood in the context of the Strong Black Woman schema, in which "trying to make a way out of no way" is upheld as a cultural virtue. Black women may also conceive of their efforts as promoting a positive image of Black womanhood for themselves and other women like them. The effort to project a certain impression to the wider world may be viewed as a form of empowerment or self-advocacy, regardless of the cost. Although psychologist Sherman James's seminal work on John Henryism recognized how this burden negatively affects Black people, many health disparities researchers are just beginning to fully document the psychological and physiological toll of these efforts on human health (James, 1994).[3]

---

[3] There is a growing body of evidence on the relationship between discrimination, stress, and telomere length (Chae et al., 2016).

Ahistoricism and Stereotyping

Stereotyping of Black women has long roots in the American polity and society. As I have outlined throughout the book, tropes about Black women's lasciviousness (e.g., the Jezebel) were used to justify rape and sexual exploitation at the hands of their overseers during slavery, the Jim Crow era, and into the present day. Other stereotypes, including the Mammy, the fat, asexual woman who embodied self-sacrifice and devotion to White families; and the Sapphire, the wise-cracking angry "sista" or "angry Black woman" have long been used to erase the contours of Black women's individuality. The stereotype of the welfare queen cast all Black women as fraudulent, undeserving users of government financial support. As Patricia Hill Collins has noted, the confluence of these negative images was not only damaging to women's self-concept but was also an effort to subordinate Black women as a whole (Collins, 2000). Perhaps in response to this dehumanization, Black women cultivated the idea of themselves as strong people who were able to "make a way out of no way," seemingly able to tackle any structural barrier with the force of their will alone (Harris-Perry, 2011). Although contemporary health disparities research does not typically consider how history and sociocultural mores affect present-day health, the findings of this book suggest that incorporating a historical view is essential to ending differences in treatment.

Against this backdrop, the women's experiences at the doctor's office and in general highlight the importance of history on contemporary health. For example, Tammy (the 37-year-old mother of three whose great-grandfather was in the Tuskegee Syphilis Study) described how her family's exploitation at the hands of predominantly White medical institutions affected her engagement with healthcare providers. Although she did not directly experience the trauma and exploitation of her great-grandfather, great-grandmother, and grandfather, she seemed to carry their wounds and subsequent distrust of medical providers through time.

Given Black people's long history of exploitation and sub-par medical treatment in the United States, Tammy's experience may illuminate a broader sense of mistrust in the Black community. In this manner, taking historical events into account as we grapple with contemporary health inequities is imperative. Although we obviously cannot change the past, acknowledging the gravity and continued importance of historic, as well as ongoing, events may serve as a form of healing. This is particularly true for people of color, who often receive the tacit message to "just get over it already." Last, we must also acknowledge how the policies of previous eras have far-reaching material consequences in the present. We need a more robust accounting of the ways structural arrangements (i.e., redlining, generations of poor medical care, employment discrimination, etc.) affect people now (Feagin & Bennefield, 2014).

Interventions: Structural Problems Require Structural Solutions

Given this backdrop, the findings of this study suggest areas for further exploration and intervention. First, because discrimination is often cast as a remnant of the United States' troubled history of settler colonialism, slavery, and Jim Crow, it is difficult to accept that discrimination persists into the present. Further, the framing of racism (and other forms of discrimination) as an individual failing of "bad" or "uneducated" people obscures the ways in which structural racism is embedded in our nation's institutions, including medical schools and healthcare settings (Feagin & Bennefield, 2014). Based on this study, I argue that a more robust and candid accounting of both explicit and implicit bias in healthcare settings, including medical schools, is long overdue. Although stereotyping and bias are enacted at the individual level, i.e., between the patient and provider, racism and sexism are structured into the society as a whole. As such, there is no reason to expect medical schools and healthcare institutions would be bastions of anti-oppressive practices.

Furthermore, although the dominant paradigm in the United States emphasizes individual choice and responsibility, the empirical evidence indicates that our neighborhoods, schools, jobs, and other structural factors of day-to-day life shape individual and population health (Gehlert et al., 2008; Marmot, 2005; Williams, Mohammed, Leavell, & Collins, 2010). Given this backdrop, many social scientists have theorized these problems in the context of social structures (e.g., social capital, power, safe neighborhoods, high-quality schools, etc.) that ostensibly give rise to healthcare inequities. Sociologists Link and Phelan (1995) first conceptualized the "fundamental causes" of the health inequities framework, which represents a significant shift in the way Americans typically think about social problems in that it emphasizes the social arrangements that cause individual-level health and social problems. This approach considers how (lack of) access to society's resources is more salient in determining health and well-being than individual-level factors like genetics and health behavior. For example, we know that living near toxic waste sites or in neighborhoods of concentrated poverty is bad for your health (Diez-Roux, 2003). In fact, the distribution of resources throughout society likely shapes health behavior at the individual level (Link & Phelan, 1995; 2002; Marmot, 2005). Although the fundamental causes theory of health inequity is well established in public health and social science, thus far it has been difficult to generate the political will to consider interventions that uphold a fundamental causes approach.

However, building on the framework's underlying premise, physicians and other scholars, including social workers,[4] have begun to advance the idea of structural competency and structural interventions. Physician social scientists Metzl and Hansen (Hansen & Metzl, 2017; Metzl & Hansen, 2014) are attempting to shift the paradigm in medical education to ensure that medical students and future physicians understand how systemic inequities affect individual health. This is a seismic shift that attempts to broaden medical student education to include social science and medical humanities in an effort to grasp the systemic and institutional nature of racism and other forms of discrimination. Hansen and Metzl define structural competency as:

> a language and theoretical framework to promote institutional intervention by clinical practitioners to improve patient and community health. . . . Structural competency thus draws on the social science, medical humanities, and public health scholarship illustrating the systemic, institutional determinants of health inequalities and therefore indicating that health disparities require institutional-level intervention for remediation. (Hansen & Metzl, 2017, p. 279)

Metzl and legal scholar Dorothy Roberts (2017) take this further to integrate the notion of structural competency with an explicit focus on racism in medical settings. For example, they note that although acknowledging the ethnic, racial, or cultural background of patients is important in clinical interactions, this approach risks relying solely on the bodies of patients and not on the structures in which they find themselves. Moreover, as I have argued throughout, situating the problem at the feet of the provider and patient alone leaves practitioners unprepared to address the biological, socioeconomic, and racial impact of unequally distributed resources like grocery stores, schools, or playgrounds while minimizing the scope and historical context of the problem.

Advancing a framework that considers institutional racism and other structural factors is a critical first step in changing medical and other forms of clinical practice, including social work. Structural competency provides a way of integrating individual processes with the macro-environmental constraints that can either facilitate or impede individual opportunity and behavior. Sociologist

---

[4] See National Association of Social Workers, *Institutional racism and the social work profession: a call to action*, http://www.socialworkers.org/diversity/institutionalracism.pdf

Hannah Bradby (2010) explains the implications of not addressing both racism and structure:

> hypothesizing mechanisms that include the micro-processes of inter-
> actions between patients and professionals and the macroprocesses of
> population-level inequalities is a missing step in our reasoning at pres-
> ent. . . . [A]s long as we see the solution to racism lying only in educat-
> ing the individual, we fail to address the complexity of racism and risk
> alienating patients and physicians alike. (as cited in Metzl & Roberts,
> 2017, p. 682)

Moreover, the structural competency framework provides concrete examples of how clinical practitioners may intervene to address the seemingly insur-
mountable problems many patients face. In addition to training practitioners to
be skeptical of race- based explanations of clinical differences, the framework
also suggests developing partnerships between doctors and other professionals
who work with the same populations. For example, physicians in Boston partnered with a legal aid group to address issues of housing insecurity among their
patients (MLPB, 2017). Another example of this kind of collaboration includes
a group of Nashville-based medical students who observed that their Black
patients were "noncompliant" with instructions to take their medication after
eating. After asking their patients why this happened, the students found that
they lived more than 2 hours from a grocery store, making medication compliance very difficult. The students partnered with a local nonprofit to deliver food
to remote areas in refrigerated trucks (Community Food Advocates, 2017).

Although structural competency represents a cohesive and thoughtful way to
both think about and act on health inequities, it is by no means a panacea. It does
not address explicit racism, misogyny, or other overt forms of discrimination in
medical or other clinical settings. Nor can it address the White supremacist and
hetero-patriarchal frame upon which the United States is founded. However, it
takes the optimistic view that if providers were more explicitly attune to structural explanations for individual problems, they would be less likely to attribute
those problems to the person's race or gender. In this manner, structural competency assumes the best of patients and providers alike.

Although we have yet to live up to the highest ideals upon which the United
States was created, we owe it to our fellow human beings to aspire to that which
has eluded us since the nation's inception. Now is the time to do the right thing.

Appendix

RESEARCH METHODS

Overall Approach

As I have argued throughout this book, although differences in treatment persist across class, there is little research about how and why this occurs. The more I reviewed health disparities research, the more I noticed a pattern in which the majority of research focused on minorities who were socioeconomically disadvantaged. Although I am deeply concerned about society's most socioeconomically vulnerable, I wanted my research to pose different but equally important questions: (1) Why do Black middle-class women continue to receive different healthcare treatment than their White counterparts? (2) Do Black middle-class women perceive that they are treated differently because of their race and gender? And, (3) do they attempt to mitigate discrimination by leveraging their material and cultural resources (e.g., ability to change doctors, ability to use medical terminology, etc.)?

Because there is relatively little research on the health of the Black middle class, or how class status may not protect Black people's health to the same extent as the White middle class, this study focused only on Black middle-class women (without a comparison group of White middle-class women). The study was also designed to better understand subtle differences between lower middle-class Black women relative to upper middle-class Black women. As such, the sample reflects intraracial class variation. For example, I interviewed a Black woman who earned six figures working in the financial services industry, whereas another women ran a small nonprofit and made less than $50,000 a year. Both of these women would be described as middle class in spite of substantive differences in income and wealth.

Furthermore, because I sought an in-depth understanding of women's healthcare experiences from their own point of view, I used qualitative methods. This approach emerges from a long line of scholarship about the Black middle class in particular, including DuBois's *The Philadelphia Negro* (1899), Frazier's *Black Bourgeoisie* (1957), Drake and Cayton's *Black Metropolis* (1945), Cose's *The Rage of a Privileged Class* (Cose, 1994), Feagin and Sikes's *Living with Racism: The Black Middle Class Experience* (1994), Pattillo's *Black Picket Fences* (1999), Lacy's *Blue-Chip Black* (2007), among many others. These books analyze the unique privileges and vulnerabilities of the Black middle class. Similar to the approach I have taken in my work, the majority of the aforementioned books explore the experiences of the Black middle class in a single city using interviews, focus groups, and other qualitative data collection techniques to capture the group's unique social position.

Analytic Strategy

To collect and analyze the focus group and interview data, I followed a particular qualitative method called *grounded theory* based on the general theoretical assumptions of the method as outlined by sociologist Kathy Charmaz (2006). Charmaz's constructivist approach departs from the method first put forth by Glaser and Strauss (1967) in which they recommended that researchers build theory from the ground up without a priori assumptions based on previous research. Charmaz's conceptualization acknowledges that most researchers have hunches about the work they do and conduct in-depth reviews of existing literature before beginning research projects. As such, Charmaz advocates using sensitizing concepts, or ideas gleaned from the review of existing research, which provide conceptual grounding while remaining open to the specific ideas raised by the women themselves.

Furthermore, following the tenets of qualitative methods, it is important for the researcher to grapple with the ways in which her own position (e.g., race, gender, sexual orientation, etc.) may affect the research process. As I noted in the introductory chapter, I am a mixed-race Black middle-class woman. Because my position as a Black middle-class woman ostensibly gave me an insider perspective, I was careful to reflect on how my position may have affected what the participants felt comfortable sharing as well as how I interpreted their responses (Lincoln, Lynham, & Guba, 2011). For example, during the recruitment process, being a Black middle-class woman made it easier to garner participation. Some women remarked that if their participation would help me complete my doctorate, they were very happy to support another Black woman to complete her education. During the interviews, women would often suggest that I understood their experiences by virtue of also being a Black middle-class woman.

Overall, I believe that sharing certain demographic characteristics with the women in the study helped me elicit their honest, unvarnished perceptions. However, it is also possible that the ostensible similarity may have precluded women from raising issues that ran counter to what they believed I wanted to hear. Although I cannot rule this out as a possibility, I feel strongly that the respondents were honest with me, even in expressing views that may have been controversial. For example, women shared their opinions about tensions in the Black community over skin color, which is a loaded and potentially very tense topic among Black women. They also described not wanting to be treated by a Black doctor because they believed they would receive poorer quality care. These topics are by no means neutral, and the women had no way of knowing where I stood on such matters. Regardless, they shared their experiences with me, suggesting that they were not bound by intraracial social conventions. Throughout the research process, I also received feedback on my interpretation of the data from my dissertation committee and a qualitative research group comprised of other doctoral students and a professor who was an expert in qualitative methods.

Data Collection

As I embarked on the study, I realized that using two different data collection methods (i.e., speaking to women one-on-one and in small groups) could provide important insights into their healthcare experiences from slightly different perspectives. As a result, I conducted focus groups as well as one-on-one interviews. The focus groups were conducted first and were designed to test and refine the questions I would ask in the subsequent interviews. In this manner, the focus groups helped me determine whether my questions passed the "laugh test" and were sufficiently credible to carry over to the one- on-one interviews. The focus groups were also an important source of data on their own.

In addition, focus groups are particularly challenging to recruit and implement. For example, simply identifying women who met the criteria of being lower middle class (e.g., had a high school degree or some college but had not completed a degree, compared to upper middle class; e.g., college or advanced degree) proved to be a challenge. Once I had identified the women and conducted a preliminary screening interview with them on the phone to determine whether they met the study's criteria, I had to ensure that a group of busy people showed up after work to discuss their healthcare experiences with total strangers. I tried to make the experience more pleasant by providing food and paying the women $25 for their time. Overall, I was able to conduct two focus groups in 1 month. Successfully carrying out the focus groups allowed me to anticipate the problems I would encounter with the recruitment and enrollment strategies for the in-depth interview participants, which is in keeping with the iterative nature of qualitative research (Denzin & Lincoln, 2011).

Focus Group Recruitment and Sample

I used multiple strategies to recruit focus group participants, including posting flyers in public spaces throughout Chicago (e.g., grocery stores, coffee shops, the Chicago Black Women's Expo, etc.). Given that identifying a group with this particular combination of race, gender, and class attributes was relatively difficult, I also asked members of my own extended network (including men and women of all backgrounds) to identify possible participants. As such, although I used acquaintances to identify possible respondents, the acquaintances were not all Black middle-class women themselves.

Therefore, I argue that this strategy did not lead me to enroll respondents who were systematically similar. Although the participants ostensibly shared the same race, class, and gender—that is, they were all Black women—they were no more similar than any other individuals would be based on those characteristics. In other words, Black women are not monolithic, and simply recruiting Black middle-class women did not lead to a systematically similar sample.

Furthermore, I purposively recruited respondents based on their educational status. Although individual measures of socioeconomic status are imperfect (Braveman et al., 2005), educational status is relatively stable over time, less likely to be influenced by health status than income or occupation, and provides a relatively simple way to categorize potential respondents (Shavers, 2007). As such, I recruited focus group participants based on their educational attainment. "Upper middle" class respondents were required to have an advanced degree (i.e., anything beyond a bachelor's degree), and women in the "lower middle" group were required to have a bachelor's degree or lower. I also conducted a follow-up screening phone call in which I asked about their profession, marital status, and whether they owned a home.

Women in the lower middle group ($n = 6$) ranged in age from 35 to 57, with an average age of 38.6. Five women had some college education. One woman in the lower middle-class focus group had a bachelor's degree, but, after conducting a follow-up phone screening, I determined that, based on other socio-economic status measures (i.e., income, home ownership, and occupation), her experience would be more accurately categorized as lower middle class. Women in the upper middle group ($n = 5$) ranged in age from 37 to 48, with an average age of 44.2. Four women had advanced degrees, while one had a bachelor's degree. The groups were conducted in 2010, in Chicago, and each lasted approximately 2 hours. As noted earlier, the focus group data were used to inform the development of the in-depth interview instrument and as a source of data on their own (Morgan & Krueger, 1998). As such, the focus groups were conducted in the months leading up to enrollment for the interviews.

I asked women in the focus groups to share their general impressions of seeking healthcare, including positive and negative experiences. Women were also asked to reflect on their most recent healthcare experience and questioned about whether they purposefully managed their persona to try to get better treatment. To tap into the energy of a group, I encouraged the women to share their experiences as a whole, not simply to report out their opinions one after another. Based on the focus group data, I developed a semi-structured interview instrument. Later, I asked women who participated in the in- depth interviews similar questions, which allowed me to compare information from the focus groups and in-depth interviews.

Interview Recruitment and Sample

Similar to recruitment for the focus groups, I recruited interview respondents through multiple mechanisms, including snowball sampling, in which I asked women already in the study to help me identify other women who might have been interested in participating. I also placed announcements on Facebook and Craigslist asking self-identified Black women living in Chicago to participate in a study about their healthcare experiences. Like the focus groups, women were initially recruited to the study based on their educational attainment. Although the definition of "middle class" is contested, many social scientists use median income, educational attainment, or individual aspirations (e.g., being able to send children to college) to categorize this group (Renwick & Short, 2014). Based on a follow-up phone screening, women were included in the study if they met one or more of the following criteria: (1) income (a household income of 50,000 or more); 2) education (having a bachelor's degree or beyond); 3) occupation (having a professional job or owning a business); and 4) home ownership. Enrollment for the study was concluded at 19 respondents because saturation of the main themes had been reached, meaning that additional interviews were not yielding new findings or thematic variation.

Table A.1 summarizes the demographic characteristics of the interview respondents.

In addition, given that people with health problems are more likely to have engaged the healthcare system, I asked each woman to rate her own health status and to disclose any serious chronic or acute illnesses/injuries she experienced as an adult. Of 19 respondents, eight had no significant health problems and rated their health as excellent or good. Six had a previous acute, serious illness like

Table A.1 **Interview respondent demographics**

	Range	#Participants	Average	Minimum	Maximum
Age	35–44	3	48.8	38	67
	45–54	7			
	55–64	8			
	65+	1			
Health insurance*	Public	4			
	Private	13			
	None	2			
Education	Some college	6			
	BA	5			
	Advanced degree	8			
Income*	<$30 k/yr	4			
	$30 k–$49,999/yr	3			
	$50 k–$99,999/yr	6			
	$100k+	4			
	Declined to state	2			
Home ownership	Own	12			
	Rent	7			
Marital status	Married	8			
	Single	4			
	Divorced	7			

*Two respondents had insurance coverage for the majority of their lives but were uninsured at the time of data collection.

breast cancer. These women also rated their current health as excellent or good. Five had chronic conditions including autoimmune diseases or work-related injuries. Women with chronic illnesses ranged in their self-reported health from good to poor.

In-Depth Interviews

I conducted individual interviews in 2010 and 2011. The interviews were conducted in the women's homes or at location of their choice and were approximately 90–120 minutes in length. I compensated each woman $25 in cash in exchange for her time.[1] The Institutional Review Board at the University of Chicago approved all study protocols. Pseudonyms were used to refer to the women throughout the book.

The semi-structured in-depth interview guide included questions and probes organized into the following categories: (1) general impressions of the health-care system and healthcare encounters; (2) race and gender preference in health-care settings; (3) racial attitudes and discrimination based on race, gender, class, and other factors; and (4) intra racial solidarity. The interview guide included questions that were adapted from Lacy (2007) about intraracial class variation and Malat and colleagues (Malat, van Ryn, & Purcell, 2006) about positive self-presentation strategies. However, the interview guide was open-ended and allowed women to bring up topics that were salient to them. Similar to the focus groups, I asked women to reflect on their experiences with healthcare providers overall, their own health status, and their experiences of discrimination, both in healthcare settings and in general. I did not specifically ask about stereotyping or cultural health capital. These concepts emerged during the analysis.

Analysis

The focus groups and in-depth interviews were audio-recorded and transcribed. The analysis was informed by grounded theory analytical techniques and texts on coding and analyzing qualitative data (Auerbach & Silverstein, 2003; Charmaz, 2006; Corbin & Strauss, 1990; Creswell, 2007; Padgett, 2008). The transcriptions of the individual interviews and the focus groups were imported into the NVivo software program, which assisted in data management. I also used Excel to organize my observations of the data and to record emergent themes. The transcripts were checked for accuracy against the audio recordings.

The second phase of data analysis included line-by-line coding on the paper copies of the transcripts and using the constant comparative method, a process in which newly collected data are compared to existing data to arrive at new codes and themes.

First, I used in vivo codes that reflected the women's own words and overall perceptions of healthcare providers. Second, based on these codes, I grouped the responses into main themes. For example, with regard to stereotype threat and the cultural health capital strategies women used to manage it, the following

---

[1] I received a small grant to offset the costs of paying women to participate in the study and to pay for interview transcription. Paying study respondents a small incentive to participate in a study is common practice in social science research.

themes emerged: (1) maintaining their appearance or physical self-presentation, (2) conducting research prior to the healthcare encounter, (3) connecting with the healthcare provider, and (4) emphasizing their professional and/or educational credentials. Last, I developed additional theoretical codes that reflected the elements of cultural health capital, including knowledge of relevant information to share with provider, ability to communicate social privilege, and others.[2] I followed this process to arrive at the main findings presented in the book. Focus group data were analyzed similarly. In addition, based on Morgan and Krueger's (1998) focus group analysis techniques, I considered the group dynamic as a whole and did not privilege individual vocal group participants in the analysis.

Limitations

Although this study has several strengths, including the novelty of collecting data from Black middle-class women and reviewing intraracial class variation, the study is limited by the following factors. First, it is very challenging to precisely define and operationalize class status, particularly given that I was concerned with relatively small gradations between upper middle and lower middle class. For example, a woman who participated in the focus groups was an entrepreneur with a high school degree, rented her home, and had a household income of over $100,000. Based on her educational attainment and lack of home ownership she would not necessarily be characterized as upper middle class. However, her household income would place her squarely in the middle to upper middle-class category. However, in her case, because I made decisions about who should be included in the focus groups based on their educational attainment, I categorized the woman as lower middle class based on her educational status alone. Based on her comments in the focus group, the woman's experience was similar to other lower middle-class women. This woman's characteristics exemplify how challenging it is to define "middle class," particularly in such fine increments of lower middle to upper middle class.

Moreover, given how challenging it is to define middle class and to assign real people to relatively fine categories, it is possible that I misclassified some of the study respondents. This could explain why I did not observe substantive differences between women who were upper middle compared to lower middle class. It is also possible that, when it comes to healthcare, race and gender are simply more salient than class. In other words, I may not have observed differences

---

[2] The codes and analytic strategy were developed in consultation with a qualitative methods working group at the University of Chicago.

in the way lower middle-class women interpreted their healthcare experiences compared to upper middle-class women simply because their experiences in that setting were shaped by being Black women regardless of class. However, although the relatively small size of the sample facilitated an in-depth understanding of this phenomenon, I cannot be sure how to interpret the similarities I observed across class. I hope to carry out further research in this area to determine the robustness of this preliminary finding.

In spite of this limitation, the findings suggest that Black women face persistent challenges in healthcare settings that are primarily related to their race and gender. Many were able to leverage their class resources to counteract biased treatment. However, it is difficult to evaluate whether they were successful in trying to mitigate discrimination or how their efforts may affect their health.

In addition, this study centers the perspectives of women who graciously shared their stories with me. In this manner, the women's perspective is privileged relative to the providers with whom they interacted. Although this was a deliberate choice, I must make it clear that I did not verify the women's accounts relative to their providers. As such, I have no way of knowing whether the provider would dispute or confirm the women's characterizations of their healthcare encounters. I am not suggesting that the women's stories are all "factual." Rather, they represent the women's "truths" as filtered through their life experiences, memories, and recollections. All told, the study may have benefited from hearing the provider's perception of events. That said, the women's interpretations of their own healthcare experiences are certainly most salient to them as individuals, and women's perspectives of their health remain shockingly absent from healthcare debates.

Last, in my effort to provide the most robust backdrop for understanding the women's experiences, I have included recent research that rounds out the overall healthcare context, including the race and gender dynamics that affect Black women in that setting. It is my hope that the empirical data, coupled with recent research, provide a comprehensive picture of the strengths and challenges Black middle-class women face in the American healthcare system.

Writing the Book

Although I completed my dissertation in 2013, I knew that to write a book I would need to return to the data with fresh eyes. I embarked on the book project in 2015, secured a book contract in the fall of 2016, and began to reanalyze the data. As I sat down over the coming months to write and review the transcripts, I found that the women were incredibly forthcoming about their stories. Rereading the transcripts of the focus groups and interviews and returning to the audio files in which I actually heard their voices brought the women back to life for me, especially their laughter, irreverence, and strength. I remembered sitting with them as they volunteered some of the most heartbreaking stories about going to the doctor or simply about living their lives as Black women. I also relived the funny and incisive moments in a focus group in which they laughed about doctors using the money they made off hysterectomies to pay the rent.

Becoming reacquainted with the data allowed me to round out their stories and bear witness to the richness of their experiences, including all of life's joys and challenges.

All told, writing the book was a rewarding and enriching experience. I hope that this review of the methods provides ample guidance for doctoral students, researchers, and other scholars to carry out the complex and illuminating challenge of qualitative research.

REFERENCES

Abell, J. E., Egan, B. M., Wilson, P. W. F., Lipsitz, S., Woolson, R. F., & Lackland, D. T. (2008). Differences in cardiovascular disease mortality associated with body mass between Black and White persons. *American Journal of Public Health, 98*(1), 63–66. https://doi.org/10.2105/AJPH.2006.093781

Acosta, D., & Ackerman-Barger, K. (2017). Breaking the silence: Time to talk about race and racism. *Academic Medicine, 92*(3), 285. https://doi.org/10.1097/ACM.0000000000001416

Alexander, M. (2010). *The New Jim Crow: Mass incarceration in the age of colorblindness.* New York: The New Press.

Anachebe, N. F. (2006). Racial and ethnic disparities in infant and maternal mortality. *Ethnicity & Disease, 16*(2 Suppl 3), S3–71–76.

Anderson, E. (2000). *Code of the street: Decency, violence, and the moral life of the inner city.* W. W. Norton & Company.

Anderson, E. (2015). The white space. *Sociology of Race and Ethnicity, 1*(1), 10–21. https://doi.org/10.1177/2332649214561306

Anderson, E., Asbury, D., Austin, D. W., Kim, E. C., Kulkarni, V. S., Anderson, E., & Kulkarni, V. S. (2012). The legacy of racial caste: An exploratory ethnography. *Annals of the American Academy of Political and Social Science, 642*(1), 25–42. https://doi.org/10.1177/0002716212437337

Aronson, J., Burgess, D., Phelan, S. M., & Juarez, L. (2013). Unhealthy interactions: The role of stereotype threat in health disparities. *American Journal of Public Health, 103*(1), 50–56.

Auerbach, C., & Silverstein, L. B. (2003). *Qualitative data: An introduction to coding and analysis.* 1st edn. New York: New York University.

Bailey, M. (2010, March 15). They aren't talking about me. Retrieved November 21, 2017 from http://www.crunkfeministcollective.com/2010/03/14/they-arent- talking-about-me/

Bailey, M. (2016). Misogynoir in medical media: On Caster Semenya and R. Kelly. *Catalyst: Feminism, Theory, Technoscience, 2*(2). Retrieved from http://catalystjournal.org/ojs/index.php/catalyst/article/view/98

Barbujani, G., Magagni, A., Minch, E., & Cavalli-Sforza, L. L. (1997). An apportionment of human DNA diversity. *Proceedings of the National Academy of Sciences, 94*(9), 4516–4519.

Barnes, L. L., Plotnikoff, G. A., Fox, K., & Pendleton, S. (2000). Spirituality, religion, and pediatrics: Intersecting worlds of healing. *Pediatrics, 106*(Suppl 3), 899–908.

Beauboeuf-Lafontant, T. (2005). Keeping up appearances, getting fed up: The embodiment of strength among African American women. *Meridians: Feminism, Race, Transnationalism, 5*(2), 104–123. https://doi.org/10.1353/mer.2005.0003

Bediako, P. T., BeLue, R., & Hillemeier, M. M. (2015). A comparison of birth outcomes among Black, Hispanic, and Black Hispanic women. *Journal of Racial and Ethnic Health Disparities*, 2(4), 573–582. https://doi.org/10.1007/s40615-015-0110-2

Benkert, R., & Peters, R. M. (2005). African American women's coping with health care prejudice. *Western Journal of Nursing Research*, 27(7), 863–889. https://doi.org/10.1177/0193945905278588

Blanchard, J., Nayar, S., & Lurie, N. (2007). Patient-provider and patient-staff racial concordance and perceptions of mistreatment in the health care setting. *Journal of General Internal Medicine*, 22(8), 1184–1189. https://doi.org/10.1007/s11606-007-0210-8

Blascovich, J., Spencer, S. J., Quinn, D., & Steele, C. (2001). African Americans and high blood pressure: The role of stereotype threat. *Psychological Science*, 12(3), 225–229. https://doi.org/10.1111/1467-9280.00340

Blau, F. D. (2016). *Gender, inequality, and wages*. New York: Oxford University Press.

Bradby, H. (2010). What do we mean by "racism?": Conceptualising the range of what we call racism in health care settings: A commentary on Peek et al. *Social Science and Medicine*, 71(1), 10–12.

Brandt, A. M. (1978). Racism and research: The case of the Tuskegee Syphilis Study. *Hastings Center Report*, 8(6), 21–29. https://doi.org/10.2307/3561468

Braveman, P., & Barclay, C. (2009). Health disparities beginning in childhood: A life-course perspective. *Pediatrics*, 124(Suppl 3), S163–S175. https://doi.org/10.1542/peds.2009-1100D

Braveman, P., Cubbin, C., Marchi, K., Egerter, S., & Chavez, G. (2001). Measuring socioeconomic status/position in studies of racial/ethnic disparities: Maternal and infant health. *Public Health Reports*, 116(5), 449.

Braveman, P. A., Cubbin, C., Egerter, S., Chideya, S., Marchi, K. S., Metzler, M., & Posner, S (2005). Socioeconomic status in health research. One size does not fit all. *JAMA*, 294, 2879–2888.

Bridges, K. (2011). *Reproducing race: An ethnography of pregnancy as a site of racialization*. Berkeley: University of California Press.

Burgess, D. J., Fu, S. S., & Van Ryn, M. (2004). Why do providers contribute to disparities and what can be done about it? *Journal of General Internal Medicine* 19(11), 1154–1159.

Burgess, D. J., Van Ryn, M., Crowley-Matoka, M., & Malat, J. (2006). Understanding the provider contribution to race/ethnicity disparities in pain treatment: Insights from dual process models of stereotyping. *Pain Medicine*, 7(2), 119–134.

Burgess, D. J., Warren, J., Phelan, S., Dovidio, J., & van Ryn, M. (2010). Stereotype threat and health disparities: What medical educators and future physicians need to know. *Journal of General Internal Medicine*, 25(Suppl 2), S169–S177. https://doi.org/10.1007/s11606-009-1221-4

Casciotti, D. M., & Klassen, A. C. (2011). Factors associated with female provider preference among African American women, and implications for breast cancer screening. *Health Care for Women International*, 32(7), 581–598. https://doi.org/10.1080/07399332.2011.565527

Cashell, B. W. (2008). Who are the "middle class"? *Federal Publications*, 554.

Centers for Disease Control and Prevention (U.S.). (2002). Morbidity and Mortality Weekly Report: Hysterectomy Surveillance in the US-1994–1999. Atlanta, GA. https://www.cdc.gov/Mmwr/preview/mmwrhtml/ss5105a1.htm

Chae, D. H., Epel, E. S., Nuru-Jeter, A. M., Lincoln, K. D., Taylor, R. J., Lin, J., & Thomas, S. B. (2016). Discrimination, mental health, and leukocyte telomere length among African American men. *Psychoneuroendocrinology*, 63, 10–16. https://doi.org/10.1016/j.psyneuen.2015.09.001

Chandler, D. (2010). The underutilization of health services in the Black community: An examination of causes and effects. *Journal of Black Studies*, 40(5), 915–931. https://doi.org/10.1177/0021934708320723

Charmaz, K. (2006). *Constructing grounded theory: A practical guide through qualitative analysis*. London: Sage Publications.

Chen, F. M., Fryer, G. E., Phillips, R. L., Wilson, E., & Pathman, D. E. (2005). Patients' beliefs about racism, preferences for physician race, and satisfaction with care. *Annals of Family Medicine, 3*(2), 138–143. https://doi.org/10.1370/afm.282

Choo, H. Y., & Ferree, M. M. (2010). Practicing intersectionality in sociological research: A critical analysis of inclusions, interactions, and institutions in the study of inequalities. *Sociological Theory, 28*(2), 129–149. https://doi.org/10.1111/j.1467-9558.2010.01370.x

Chowkwanyun, M. (2011). The strange disappearance of history from racial health disparities research. *Du Bois Review: Social Science Research on Race, 8*(1), 253–270. https://doi.org/10.1017/S1742058X11000142

Cikara, M., Bruneau, E., Van Bavel, J. J., & Saxe, R. (2014). Their pain gives us pleasure: How intergroup dynamics shape empathic failures and counter-empathic responses. *Journal of Experimental Social Psychology, 55*, 110–125.

Clark, R., Anderson, N. B., Clark, V. R., & Williams, D. R. (1999). Racism as a stressor for African Americans: A biopsychosocial model. *American Psychologist, 54*, 10.

Cohen, C. J. (1999). *The boundaries of blackness: AIDS and the breakdown of Black politics.* Chicago: University of Chicago Press.

Cole, E. R., & Omari, S. R. (2003). Race, class and the dilemmas of upward mobility for African Americans. *Journal of Social Issues, 59*(4), 785–802. https://doi.org/10.1046/j.0022-4537.2003.00090.x

Collins, P. H. (2000). *Black feminist thought: Knowledge, consciousness, and the politics of empowerment.* New York: Routledge.

Combahee River Collective. (1977). *A black feminist statement* (pp. 210–218). https://combaheerivercollective.weebly.com/the-combahee-river-collective-statement.html

Community Food Advocates. (2017). *Food sharing.* Retrieved December 7, 2017, from http://www.communityfoodadvocates.org/category/food-sharing/

Conley, D. (2010). *Being Black, living in the red: Race, wealth, and social policy in America.* Berkeley: University of California Press.

Conrad, S., Xierali, I., Zhang, K., Arceneaux, T., Peters, L., & Dill, M. (2014). *Diversity in the physician workforce: Facts & figures* (Facts & Figures Data Series No. 18). AAMC Center for Workforce Studies. Retrieved from http://aamcdiversityfactsandfigures.org/section-ii-current-status-of-us-physician- workforce/

Cooper, L. A., Roter, D. L., Johnson, R. L., Ford, D. E., Steinwachs, D. M., & Powe, N. R. (2003). Patient-centered communication, ratings of care, and concordance of patient and physician race. *Annals of Internal Medicine, 139*(11), 907–915.

Cooper, R. S., Kennelly, J., R., Durazo-Arvizu, R., Oh, H.-J., Kaplan, G., & Lynch, J. (2001). Relationship between premature mortality and socioeconomic factors in Black and White populations of US metropolitan areas. *Public Health Reports, 116*(5), 464–473. https://doi.org/10.1093/phr/116.5.464

Conley, D. (1999). Being Black. *Living in the Red: Race, Wealth, and Social Policy in America.*

Corbin, J., & Strauss, A. (1990). *Basics of qualitative research: Grounded theory procedures and techniques* (S. Oaks, Ed.). Thousand Oaks, CA: Sage Publications.

Cose, E. (1994). *The rage of a privileged class: Why do prosperous Blacks still have the blues?* New York: Harper Collins.

Crenshaw, K. (1991). Mapping the margins: Intersectionality, identity politics, and violence against women of color. *Stanford Law Review, 43*(6), 1241–1299.

Creswell, J. W. (2007). *Qualitative inquiry and research design: Choosing among five approaches,* 2nd edn. Thousand Oaks, CA: Sage Publications.

Dale, H. E., Polivka, B. J., Chaudry, R. V., & Simmonds, G. C. (2010). What young African American women want in a health care provider. *Qualitative Health Research, 20*(11), 1484–1490. https://doi.org/10.1177/1049732310374043

David, R., & Collins, J. (2007). Disparities in infant mortality: What's genetics got to do with it? *American Journal of Public Health, 97*(7), 1191–1197. https://doi.org/10.2105/AJPH.2005.068387

Deaton, A. (2002). Policy implications of the gradient of health and wealth. *Health Affairs*, 21(2), 13–30. https://doi.org/10.1377/hlthaff.21.2.13

Denzin, N. K., & Lincoln, Y. S. (2011). *The Sage handbook of qualitative research*. Thousand Oaks, CA: Sage.

Diez-Roux, A. (2003). The examination of neighborhood effects on health: Conceptual and methodological issues related to the presence of multiple levels of organization. In I. Kawachi & L. Berkman (Eds.), *Neighborhoods and Health* (pp. 45–64). New York, NY: Oxford University Press.

Dittmer, J. (2017). *The good doctors: The Medical Committee for Human Rights and the struggle for social justice in health care*. Jackson: University Press of Mississippi.

Drake, S. C., & Cayton, H. (1945). *Black metropolis: A study of Negro life in a northern city.* 2 vols. New York: Harper& Row.

Downey, M. M., Arteaga, S., Villaseñor, E., & Gomez, A. M. (2017). More than a destination: Contraceptive decision making as a journey. *Women's Health Issues*, 27(5), 539–545. https://doi.org/10.1016/j.whi.2017.03.004

Dubbin, L. A., Chang, J. S., & Shim, J. K. (2013). Cultural health capital and the interactional dynamics of patient-centered care. *Social Science & Medicine*, 93, 113–120.

DuBois, W. E. B. (1903). *The souls of Black folk: Essays and sketches*. Chicago: A. C. McClurg & Company.

DuBois, W. E. B., & Eaton, I. (1899). *The Philadelphia Negro: A social study*. Published for the University.

Duster, T. (2005). Medicine, race and reification in science. *Science (New York, N. ''Y.)*, 307(5712), 1050–1051. https://doi.org/10.1126/science.1110303

Earnshaw, V. A., Rosenthal, L., Carroll-Scott, A., Santilli, A., Gilstad-Hayden, K., & Ickovics, J. R. (2016). Everyday discrimination and physical health: Exploring mental health processes. *Journal of Health Psychology*, 21(10), 2218–2228. https://doi.org/10.1177/1359105315572456

Eltoukhi, H. M., Modi, M. N., Weston, M., Armstrong, A. Y., & Stewart, E. A. (2014). The health disparities of uterine fibroids for African American women: A public health issue. *American Journal of Obstetrics and Gynecology*, 210(3), 194–199. https://doi.org/10.1016/j.ajog.2013.08.008

Fanon, F. (1952). *Black skin White masks*. New York: Grove Press.

Farmer, M. M., & Ferraro, K. F. (2005). Are racial disparities in health conditional on socioeconomic status? *Social Science & Medicine*, 60(1), 191–204. https://doi.org/10.1016/j.socscimed.2004.04.026

Feagin, J., & Bennefield, Z. (2014). Systemic racism and US health care. *Social Science & Medicine*, 103(Suppl C), 7–14. https://doi.org/10.1016/j.socscimed.2013.09.006

Feagin, J. R., & Sikes, M. P. (1994). *Living with racism: The Black middle-class experience*. Boston: Beacon Press.

FitzGerald, C., & Hurst, S. (2017). Implicit bias in healthcare professionals: A systematic review. *BMC Medical Ethics*, 18, 19. https://doi.org/10.1186/s12910-017-0179-8

Ford, C. L. (2016). Critical race theory and empirical methods public health critical race praxis: An introduction, an intervention, and three points for consideration. *Wis. L. Rev.*, 2016, 477–655.

Foucault, M. (1977). *Discipline and punish: The birth of the prison*. New York: Knopf Doubleday Publishing Group.

Frazier, F. (1957). *Black bourgeoisie*. New York: Simon and Schuster.

Frost, D. M. (2011). Social stigma and its consequences for the socially stigmatized. *Social and Personality Psychology Compass*, 5(11), 824–839. https://doi.org/10.1111/j.1751-9004.2011.00394.x

Gamble, V. N. (1993). A legacy of distrust: African Americans and medical research. *American Journal of Preventive Medicine*, 9(6 Suppl), 35–38.

Gehlert, S., Sohmer, D., Sacks, T., Mininger, C., McClintock, M., & Olopade, O. (2008). Targeting health disparities: A model linking upstream determinants to downstream interventions. *Health Affairs, 27*(2), 339–349. https://doi.org/10.1377/hlthaff.27.2.339

Geronimus, A. T. (1996). Black/white differences in the relationship of maternal age to birthweight: A population-based test of the weathering hypothesis. *Social Science & Medicine, 42*(4), 589–597.

Geronimus, A. T., Hicken, M. T., Pearson, J. A., Seashols, S. J., Brown, K. L., & Cruz, T. D. (2010). Do US Black women experience stress-related accelerated biological aging? *Human Nature, 21*(1), 19–38. https://doi.org/10.1007/s12110-010-9078-0

Giger, J. N., Appel, S. J., Davidhizar, R., & Davis, C. (2008). Church and spirituality in the lives of the African American community. *Journal of Transcultural Nursing, 19*(4), 375–383. https://doi.org/10.1177/1043659608322502

Gilens, M. (1998). Racial attitudes and race-neutral social policies: White opposition to welfare and the politics of racial inequality. *Perception and Prejudice: Race and Politics in the United States,* 171–201.

Gilens, M. (2003). How the poor became black. In S. F. Schram (Ed.), *Race and the politics of welfare reform* (pp. 101–130). Lansing: University of Michigan Press.

Gilens, M. (2009). *Why Americans hate welfare: Race, media, and the politics of antipoverty policy.* Chicago: University of Chicago Press.

Gilmore, R. W. (2007). *Golden gulag: Prisons, surplus, crisis, and opposition in globalizing California.* Berkeley: University of California Press.

Gilroy, P. (1993). *The black Atlantic: Modernity and double consciousness.* Cambridge, MA: Harvard University Press.

Giscombé, C. L., & Lobel, M. (2005). Explaining disproportionately high rates of adverse birth outcomes among African Americans: The impact of stress, racism, and related factors in pregnancy. *Psychological Bulletin, 131*(5), 662–683. https://doi.org/10.1037/0033-2909.131.5.662

Glaser, B., & Strauss, A. (1967). Grounded theory: The discovery of grounded theory. *Sociology, 12,* 27–49.

Goffman, E. (1959). *The presentation of self in everyday life.* New York: Anchor.

Gould, S. J. (1996). *The mismeasure of man.* New York: WW Norton & Company.

Goyal, M. K., Kuppermann, N., Cleary, S. D., Teach, S. J., & Chamberlain, J. M. (2015). Racial disparities in pain management of children with appendicitis in emergency departments. *JAMA Pediatrics, 169*(11), 996–1002. https://doi.org/10.1001/jamapediatrics.2015.1915

Graves Jr., J. L., & Graves, J. L. (2003). *The emperor's new clothes: Biological theories of race at the millennium.* New Brunswick, NJ: Rutgers University Press.

Gustafson, K. (2009). The criminalization of poverty. *Journal of Criminal Law and Criminology,* 643–716.

Hagiwara, N., Penner, L. A., Gonzalez, R., Eggly, S., Dovidio, J. F., Gaertner, S. L., . . . Albrecht, T. L. (2013). Racial attitudes, physician–patient talk time ratio, and adherence in racially discordant medical interactions. *Social Science & Medicine, 87*(Suppl C), 123–131. https://doi.org/10.1016/j.socscimed.2013.03.016

Hall, W. J., Chapman, M. V., Lee, K. M., Merino, Y. M., Thomas, T. W., Payne, B. K., & Coyne-Beasley, T. (2015). Implicit racial/ethnic bias among healthcare professionals and its influence on healthcare outcomes: A systematic review. *American Journal of Public Health, 105*(12), 60–76.

Hancock, A.-M. (2004). *The politics of disgust: The public identity of the welfare queen.* New York: New York University Press.

Hansen, H., & Metzl, J. M. (2017). New medicine for the US health care system: Training physicians for structural interventions. *Academic Medicine, 92*(3), 279. https://doi.org/10.1097/ACM.0000000000001542

Harrell, J. P., Hall, S., & Taliaferro, J. (2003). Physiological responses to racism and discrimination: An assessment of the evidence. *American Journal of Public Health, 93*(2), 243–248. https://doi.org/10.2105/AJPH.93.2.243

Harris, R., Tobias, M., Jeffreys, M., Waldegrave, K., Karlsen, S., & Nazroo, J. (2006). Racism and health: The relationship between experience of racial discrimination and health in New Zealand. *Social Science & Medicine (1982), 63*(6), 1428–1441. https://doi.org/10.1016/j.socscimed.2006.04.009

Harris-Perry, M. (2011). *Sister citizen: Shame, stereotypes, and black women in America.* New Haven, CT: Yale University Press.

Hatch, A. R. (2016). *Blood sugar: Racial pharmacology and food justice in Black America.* Minneapolis: University of Minnesota Press.

Havekes, E., Bader, M., & Krysan, M. (2016). Realizing racial and ethnic neighborhood preferences? Exploring the mismatches between what people want, where they search, and where they live. *Population Research and Policy Review, 35*(1), 101–126. https://doi.org/10.1007/s11113-015-9369-6

Hellwege, J. N., Jeff, J. M., Wise, L. A., Gallagher, C. S., Wellons, M., Hartmann, K. E., Velez Edwards, D. R. (2017). A multi-stage genome-wide association study of uterine fibroids in African Americans. *Human Genetics, 136*(10), 1363–1373. https://doi.org/10.1007/s00439-017-1836-1

Hershman, D., McBride, R., Jacobson, J. S., Lamerato, L., Roberts, K., Grann, V. R., & Neugut, A. I. (2005). Racial disparities in treatment and survival among women with early-stage breast cancer. *Journal of Clinical Oncology, 23*(27), 6639–6646. https://doi.org/10.1200/JCO.2005.12.633

Hicken, M., Gragg, R., & Hu, H. (2011). How cumulative risks warrant a shift in our approach to racial health disparities: the case of lead, stress, and hypertension. *Health Affairs, 30*(10), 1895–1901.

Hoberman, J. M. (2005). The primitive pelvis. The role of racial folklore in obstetrics and gynecology during the twentieth century. *Body Parts. British Explorations in Corporeality*, Forth & Crozier (Eds.), Lanham, Lexington Books, 85–104.

Hoberman, J. M. (2007). Medical racism and the rhetoric of exculpation: How do physicians think about race? *New Literary History, 38*(3), 505–525. https://doi.org/10.1353/nlh.2007.0041

Hoberman, J. (2012). *Black and blue: The origins and consequences of medical racism.* Berkeley: University of California Press.

Hobson, J. (Ed.). (2016). *Are all the women still White? Rethinking race, expanding feminisms.* New York: SUNY Press.

Hoffman, K. M., Trawalter, S., Axt, J. R., & Oliver, M. N. (2016). Racial bias in pain assessment and treatment recommendations, and false beliefs about biological differences between blacks and whites. *Proceedings of the National Academy of Sciences, 113*(16), 4296–4301. https://doi.org/10.1073/pnas.1516047113

Hollinger, D. A. (2003). Amalgamation and hypodescent: The question of ethnoracial mixture in the history of the United States. *American Historical Review, 108*(5), 1363–1390. https://doi.org/10.1086/529971

Hudson, D. L., Bullard, K. M., Neighbors, H. W., Geronimus, A. T., Yang, J., & Jackson, J. S. (2012). Are benefits conferred with greater socioeconomic position undermined by racial discrimination among African American men? *Journal of Men's Health, 9*(2), 127–136. https://doi.org/10.1016/j.jomh.2012.03.006

Hudson, D. L., Neighbors, H. W., Geronimus, A. T., & Jackson, J. S. (2016). Racial discrimination, John Henryism, and depression among African Americans. *Journal of Black Psychology, 42*(3), 221–243.

Institute of Medicine. (2009). *Initial national priorities for comparative effectiveness research.* https://doi.org/10.17226/12648

Isaacs, S. L., & Schroeder, S. A. (2004). Class—the ignored determinant of the nation's health. *The New England Journal of Medicine, 351*(11), 1137–1142. http://dx.doi.org/10.1056/NEJMsb040329

Jackson, C. L., Wang, N.-Y., Yeh, H.-C., Szklo, M., Dray-Spira, R., & Brancati, F. L. (2014). Body-mass index and mortality risk in US Blacks compared to Whites. *Obesity (Silver Spring, Md.), 22*(3), 842–851. https://doi.org/10.1002/oby.20471

Jackson, P. B., & Cummings, J. (2011). Health disparities and the black middle class: Overview, empirical findings. In B. A. Pescosolido, J. K. Martin, J. D. McLeod, & A. Rogers (Eds.), *Handbook of the sociology of health, illness, and healing* (pp. 383–410). New York: Springer.

Jackson, P. B., & Williams, D. R. (2006). The intersection of race, gender, and SES: Health paradoxes. In A. J. Schulz & L. Mullings (Eds.), *Gender, race, class, & health: Intersectional approaches* (pp. 131–162). San Francisco: Jossey-Bass.

Jacobs, E. A., Rolle, I., Ferrans, C. E., Whitaker, E. E., & Warnecke, R. B. (2006). Understanding African Americans' views of the trustworthiness of physicians. *Journal of General Internal Medicine, 21*(6), 642–647. https://doi.org/10.1111/j.1525-1497.2006.00485.x

James, S. A. (1994). John Henryism and the health of African-Americans. *Culture, Medicine and Psychiatry, 18*(2), 163–182. https://doi.org/10.1007/BF01379448

James, S. A., Strogatz, D. S., Wing, S. B., & Ramsey, D. L. (1987). Socioeconomic status, John Henryism, and hypertension in blacks and whites. *American Journal of Epidemiology, 126*(4), 664–673. https://doi.org/10.1093/oxfordjournals.aje.a114706

Jones, C., & Shorter-Gooden, K. (2003). *Shifting: The double lives of Black women in America.* New York: Haper Collins.

Jones, J. H. (1993). *Bad blood.* New York: Simon and Schuster.

Kahn, J. (2013). *Race in a bottle: The story of BiDil and racialized medicine in a post-genomic age.* New York: Columbia University Press.

Kaiser Family Foundation. (2017). *State health facts: Distribution of physicians by gender.* Retrieved from https://www.kff.org/other/state- indicator/physicians-by gender

King, A. (2016, May 30). 10 things every black girl has experienced at the hair salon. Retrieved December 28, 2017, from https://www.theodysseyonline.com/10-things-every-black-girl-has-experienced-at-the-hair-salon

Kochhar, R., Fry, R., Taylor, P., Velasco, G., & Motel, S. (2011). *Wealth gaps rise to record highs between Whites, Blacks and Hispanics.* Washington, DC: Pew Research Center, p. 37.

Koenig, B. A., Lee, S. S.-J., & Richardson, S. S. (2008). *Revisiting race in a genomic age.* New Brunswick, NJ: Rutgers University Press.

Kramer, M. R., Hogue, C. J., Dunlop, A. L., & Menon, R. (2011). Preconceptional stress and racial disparities in preterm birth: An overview. *Acta Obstetricia Et Gynecologica Scandinavica, 90*(12), 1307–1316. https://doi.org/10.1111/j.1600-0412.2011.01136.x

Krieger, N. (1987). Shades of Difference: Theoretical underpinnings of the medical controversy on Black/White Differences in the United States, 1830–1870. *International Journal of Health Services, 17*(2), 259–278. https://doi.org/10.2190/DBY6-VDQ8-HME8-ME3R

Krieger, N. (2001a). The ostrich, the albatross, and public health: An ecosocial perspective—or why an explicit focus on health consequences of discrimination and deprivation is vital for good science and public health practice. *Public Health Reports, 116*(5), 419–423.

Krieger, N. (2001b). Theories for social epidemiology in the 21st century: An ecosocial perspective. *Epidemiologic Reviews, 30*(4), 668–677.

Krieger, N. (2002). Is breast cancer a disease of affluence, poverty, or both? The case of African American women. *American Journal of Public Health, 92*(4), 611–613.

Krieger, N. (2005). Embodying inequality: A review of concepts, measures, and methods for studying health consequences of discrimination. *Embodying Inequality: Epidemiologic Perspectives,* 101–158.

Krieger, N., & Sidney, S. (1996). Racial discrimination and blood pressure: The CARDIA study of young black and white adults. *American Journal of Public Health, 86*(10), 1370–1378.

Kwate, N. O. A., & Meyer, I. H. (2011). On sticks and stones and broken bones. *Du Bois Review*, *8*(1), 191–198.

Lacy, K. R. (2007). *Blue-chip black: Race, class, and status in the new black middle class*. Berkeley: University of California Press.

Landry, B. (1987). *The new Black middle class*. Berkeley: University of California Press.

Lareau, A., & Conley, D. (Eds.). (2008). *Social class: How does it work?*. Russell Sage Foundation.

LaVeist, T. A., & Nuru-Jeter, A. (2002). Is doctor-patient race concordance associated with greater satisfaction with care? *Journal of Health and Social Behavior*, *43*(3), 296–306. https://doi.org/10.2307/3090205

LaVeist, T. A., Nuru-Jeter, A., & Jones, K. E. (2003). The association of doctor-patient race concordance with health services utilization. *Journal of Public Health Policy*, *24*(3–4), 312–323.

Lee, B. A., & Hughes, L. A. (2015). Bucking the trend: Is ethnoracial diversity declining in American communities? *Population Research and Policy Review*, *34*(1), 113–139. https://doi.org/10.1007/s11113-014-9343-8

Lee, C. I., & Jarvik, J. G. (2014). Patient-centered outcomes research in radiology: Trends in funding and methodology. *Academic Radiology*, *21*(9), 1156–1161. https://doi.org/10.1016/j.acra.2014.01.027

Lee, H., & Hicken, M. T. (2016). Death by a thousand cuts: The health implications of Black respectability politics. *Souls*, *18*(2–4), 421–445. https://doi.org/10.1080/10999949.2016.1230828

Leeds Craig, M. (2002). *Ain't I a beauty queen?: Black women, beauty, and the politics of race*. New York: Oxford University Press.

Leeds Craig, M. (2009). *The color of an ideal Negro beauty queen: Miss bronze 1961–1968: Shades of difference*. Stanford, CA: Stanford University Press.

Lewontin, R. C. (1972). The apportionment of human diversity. In T. Dobzhansky, M. K. Hecht, & W. C. Steere (Eds.), *Evolutionary biology* (pp. 381–398). Boston: Springer. https://doi.org/10.1007/978-1-4684-9063-3_14

Lincoln, Y. S., Lynham, S. A., & Guba, E. G. (2011). Paradigmatic controversies, contradictions, and emerging confluences, revisited. In N. K. Denzin & Y. S. Lincoln (Eds.), *The Sage Handbook of Qualitative Research*, *4*, 97–128. Thousand Oaks, California: Sage.

Link, B. G., & Phelan, J. (1995). Social conditions as fundamental causes of disease. *Journal of Health and Social Behavior*, Extra Issue. 80–94.

Link, B. G., & Phelan, J. C. (2002). McKeown and the idea that social conditions are fundamental causes of disease. *American Journal of Public Health*, *92*(5), 730–732. https://doi.org/10.2105/AJPH.92.5.730

Litwack, L. F. (1999). *Trouble in mind: Black southerners in the age of Jim Crow*. New York: Vintage Books.

Malat, J. R., van Ryn, M., & Purcell, D. (2006). Race, socioeconomic status, and the perceived importance of positive self-presentation in healthcare. *Social Science & Medicine*, *62*(10), 2479–2488.

Malat, J., & van Ryn, M. (2005). African-American preference for same-race healthcare providers: The role of healthcare discrimination. *Ethnicity and Disease*, *15*(4), 740.

Marks, J. (1995). *Human Biodiversity: Genes, race, and history*. Berlin: Walter De Gruyter.

Marmot, M. (2005). Social determinants of health inequalities. *Lancet*, *365*(9464), 1099–1104. https://doi.org/10.1016/S0140-6736(05)71146-6

Marmot, M. G., Kogevinas, M., & Elston, M. A. (1987). Social/economic status and disease. *Annual Review of Public Health*, *8*(1), 111–135. https://doi.org/10.1146/annurev.pu.08.050187.000551

Martin, J. L., & Yeung, K.-T. (2003). The use of the conceptual category of race in American sociology, 1937–99. *Sociological Forum*, *18*, 521–543). Retrieved from http://www.springerlink.com/index/T576181368457570.pdf

Massey, D. S., & Denton, N. A. (1993). *American apartheid: Segregation and the making of the underclass*. Harvard University Press.

Mathews, T. J., MacDorman, M. F., & Thoma, M. E. (2015). Infant mortality statistics from the 2013 period linked birth/infant death data set. *National Vital Statistics Reports, 64*(9). Hyattsville, MD: National Center for Health Statistics. https://stacks.cdc.gov/view/cdc/32752

McEwen, B. S., & Seeman, T. (1999). Protective and damaging effects of mediators of stress: Elaborating and testing the concepts of allostasis and allostatic load. *Annals of the New York Academy of Sciences, 896*(1), 30–47.

McGuire, D. L. (2010). *At the dark end of the street: Black women, rape, and resistance—A new history of the civil rights movement from Rosa Parks to the rise of Black Power.* New York: Knopf Doubleday.

McNeil, D. G. (2010). US apologizes for syphilis tests in Guatemala. *New York Times.* https://www.nytimes.com/2010/10/02/health/research/02infect.html

Meghani, S. H., Brooks, J. M., Gipson-Jones, T., Waite, R., Whitfield-Harris, L., & Deatrick, J. A. (2009). Patient–provider race-concordance: Does it matter in improving minority patients' health outcomes? *Ethnicity & Health, 14*(1), 107–130. https://doi.org/10.1080/13557850802227031

Metzl, J. M. (2010). *The protest psychosis: How schizophrenia became a Black disease.* Boston: Beacon Press.

Metzl, J. M., & Hansen, H. (2014). Structural competency: Theorizing a new medical engagement with stigma and inequality. *Social Science & Medicine, 103*(126), 133.

Metzl, J. M., & Roberts, D. E. (2017). Structural competency meets structural racism: race, politics, and the structure of medical knowledge. *The virtual mentor. VM, 16*(9), 674.

MLPB. (2017). Medical-legal partnership, Boston. Retrieved December 18, 2017, from http://www.mlpboston.org

Morgan, D. L., & Krueger, R. A. (1998). *The focus group tool kit.* Thousand Oaks, CA: Sage.

Morning, A. (2008). Reconstructing race in science and society: Biology textbooks, 1952–2002. *American Journal of Sociology, 114*(S1), S106–S137.

Morning, A. (2011). *The nature of race: How scientists think and teach about human difference.* Berkeley: University of California Press.

Mullings, L., & Wali, A. (2001). *Stress and resilience: The social context of reproduction in central Harlem.* Boston: Springer Science & Business Media.

Nelson, A. R., Stith, A. Y., & Smedley, B. D. (Eds.). (2002). *Unequal treatment: Confronting racial and ethnic disparities in health care.* Washington, DC: National Academies Press.

Nelson, T., Cardemil, E. V., & Adeoye, C. T. (2016). Rethinking strength: Black women's perceptions of the "Strong Black Woman" role. *Psychology of Women Quarterly, 40*(4), 551–563. https://doi.org/10.1177/0361684316646716

Nuru-Jeter, A., Dominguez, T. P., Hammond, W. P., Leu, J., Skaff, M., Egerter, S., . . . Braveman, P. (2009). "It's the skin you're in": African-American women talk about their experiences of racism. An exploratory study to develop measures of racism for birth outcome studies. *Maternal and Child Health Journal, 13*(1), 29. https://doi.org/10.1007/s10995-008-0357-x

Obasogie, O. K., Harris-Wai, J. N., Darling, K., Keagy, C., & Levesque, M. (2014). Race in the life sciences: An empirical assessment, 1950–2000 symposium: Critical race theory and empirical methods conference. *Fordham Law Review, 83*, 3089–3154.

Ogden, C. L., Carroll, M. D., Fryar, C. D., & Flegal, K. M. (2015). Prevalence of obesity among adults and youth: United States, 2011–2014. *NCHS Data Brief, 219*(219), 1–8.

Oliver, M. L., & Shapiro, T. M. (2006). *Black wealth, White wealth: A new perspective on racial inequality.* New York: Taylor & Francis.

Omi, M., & Winant, H. (1994). *Racial formation in the United States: From the 1960s to the 1990s* (2nd edn). New York: Routledge.

Osterman, M. J., & Martin, J. A. (2014). Trends in low-risk cesarean delivery in the United States, 1990–2013. *National Vital Statistics Reports, 63*(6).

Padgett, D. K. (2008). *Qualitative methods in social work research.* Thousand Oaks, CA: Sage Publications.

Pascoe, E. A., & Smart Richman, L. (2009). Perceived discrimination and health: A meta-analytic review. *Psychological Bulletin, 135*(4), 531–554. https://doi.org/10.1037/a0016059

Pattillo, M. (2005). Black middle-class neighborhoods. *Annual Review of Sociology, 31*(1), 305–329. https://doi.org/10.1146/annurev.soc.29.010202.095956

Pattillo, M. (2013). *Black picket fences, second edition: Privilege and peril among the Black middle class.* Chicago: University of Chicago Press.

Penner, L. A., Dovidio, J. F., West, T. V., Gaertner, S. L., Albrecht, T. L., Dailey, R. K., & Markova, and T. (2010). Aversive racism and medical interactions with Black patients: A field study. *Journal of Experimental Social Psychology, 46*(2), 436–440.

Pew Research Center. (2015). *The American Middle Class Is Losing Ground: No longer the majority and falling behind financially.* Washington, D.C.: December.

Phelan, J. C., Link, B. G., & Tehranifar, P. (2010). Social conditions as fundamental causes of health inequalities: Theory, evidence, and policy implications. *Journal of Health and Social Behavior, 51*(Suppl 1), S28–S40. https://doi.org/10.1177/0022146510383498

Pollack, C. E., Chideya, S., Cubbin, C., Williams, B., Dekker, M., & Braveman, P. (2007). Should health studies measure wealth?: A systematic review. *American Journal of Preventive Medicine, 33*(3), 250–264. https://doi.org/10.1016/j.amepre.2007.04.033

Reeder-Hayes, K. E., & Anderson, B. O. (2017). Breast cancer disparities at home and abroad: A review of the challenges and opportunities for system-level change. *Clinical Cancer Research, 23*(11), 2655–2664. https://doi.org/10.1158/1078-0432.CCR-16-2630

Renwick, T., & Short, K. (2014). *Examining the middle class in the United States using the lens of the supplemental poverty measure.* US Census Bureau Working Paper. Retrieved from https://www.census.gov/hhes/povmeas/publications/other/renwick_short-SPM.pdf

Reverby, S. M. (2001). More than fact and fiction. Cultural memory and the Tuskegee Syphilis Study. *The Hastings Center Report, 31*(5), 22–28.

Reverby, S. M. (2008). "Special treatment": BiDil, Tuskegee, and the logic of race. *Journal of Law, Medicine & Ethics, 36*(3), 478–484. https://doi.org/10.1111/j.1748- 720X.2008.294.x

Reverby, S. M. (2011). "Normal exposure" and inoculation syphilis: A PHS "Tuskegee" doctor in Guatemala, 1946–1948. *Journal of Policy History, 23*(1), 6–28.

Reverby, S. M. (2012). *Tuskegee's truths: Rethinking the Tuskegee Syphilis Study.* Chapel Hill: University of North Carolina Press Books.

Roberts, D. (1997). *Killing the Black body: Race, reproduction, and the meaning of liberty* New York: Vintage.

Rosenfeld, A. (1999). The journalist's role in bioethics. *Journal of Medicine and Philosophy, 24*(2), 108–129. https://doi.org/10.1076/jmep.24.2.108.2532

Rothblum, E. D., & Solovay, S. (Eds.). (2009). *The fat studies reader.* New York: New York University Press.

Sacks, T. K. (2013). Race and gender concordance: Strategy to reduce healthcare disparities or red herring? Evidence from a qualitative study. *Race and Social Problems, 5*(2), 88–99. https://doi.org/10.1007/s12552-013-9093-y

Sacks, T. K. (2017). Performing Black womanhood: A qualitative study of stereotypes and the healthcare encounter. *Critical Public Health,* 1–11. https://doi.org/10.1080/09581596.2017.1307323

Samuels, G. M., & Ross-Sheriff, F. (2008). Identity, oppression, and power: Feminisms and inter-sectionality theory. *Affilia, 23*(1), 5–9.

Sawyer, P. J., Major, B., Casad, B. J., Townsend, S. S. M., & Mendes, W. B. (2012). Discrimination and the stress response: Psychological and physiological consequences of anticipating prejudice in interethnic interactions. *American Journal of Public Health, 102*(5), 1020–1026. https://doi.org/10.2105/AJPH.2011.300620

Saydah, S., Imperatore, G., Cheng, Y., Geiss, L. S., & Albright, A. (2017). Disparities in diabetes deaths among children and adolescents—United States, 2000–2014. *MMWR. Morbidity and Mortality Weekly Report, 66*(19), 502–505. https://doi.org/10.15585/mmwr.mm6619a4

Schinkel, S., Schouten, B. C., Street, R. L. Jr., van den Putte, B., & van Weert, J. C. M. (2016). Enhancing health communication outcomes among ethnic minority patients: The effects of the match between participation preferences and perceptions and doctor–patient concordance. *Journal of Health Communication*, 21(12), 1251–1259. https://doi.org/10.1080/10810730.2016.1240269

Shakir, M. (2011). *Ancestral voices of the living, rise-up and claim your bird of passage: An oral history with Tuskegee-Macon county women descendants of the US Public Health Service Syphilis Study.* United States. Retrieved from https://search.proquest.com/openview/91057bc330404dac249461b5d8426bb4/1?pq- origsite=gscholar&cbl=18750&diss=y

Shapiro, T. M. (2004). *The hidden cost of being African American: How wealth perpetuates inequality.* New York: Oxford University Press.

Shavers, V. L. (2007). Measurement of socioeconomic status in health disparities research. *Journal of the National Medical Association*, 99(9), 1013.

Shen, M. J., Peterson, E. B., Costas-Muñiz, R., Hernandez, M. H., Jewell, S. T., Matsoukas, K., & Bylund, C. L. (2017). The effects of race and racial concordance on patient-physician communication: A systematic review of the literature. *Journal of Racial and Ethnic Health Disparities*, 1–24. https://doi.org/10.1007/s40615-017-0350-4

Shim, J. K. (2010). Cultural health capital a theoretical approach to understanding healthcare interactions and the dynamics of unequal treatment. *Journal of Health and Social Behavior*, 51(1), 1–15.

Steele, C. M. (1997). A threat in the air: How stereotypes shape intellectual identity and performance. *American Psychologist*, 52(6), 613–629.

Steele, C. M. (2011). *Whistling Vivaldi: How stereotypes affect us and what we can do.* New York: W. W. Norton & Company.

Steele, C. M., & Aronson, J. (1995). Stereotype threat and the intellectual test performance of African Americans. *Journal of Personality and Social Psychology*, 69(5), 797–811.

Stepan, N. (1982). *The idea of race in science: Great Britain, 1800–1960.* New York: Macmillan Press.

Sternthal, M. J., Slopen, N., & Williams, D. R. (2011). Racial disparities in health: how much does stress really matter?. *Du Bois Review: Social Science Research on Race*, 8(1), 95–113.

Sweeney, C. F., Zinner, D., Rust, G., & Fryer, G. E. (2016). Race/ethnicity and health care communication: Does patient-provider concordance matter? *Medical Care*, 54(11), 1005. https://doi.org/10.1097/MLR.0000000000000578

Taran, F. A., Brown, H. L., & Stewart, E. A. (2010). Racial diversity in uterine leiomyoma clinical studies. *Fertility and Sterility*, 94(4), 1500–1503. https://doi.org/10.1016/j.fertnstert.2009.08.037

Thomas, C. S. (2015). A new look at the black middle class: research trends and challenges. *Sociological Focus*, 48(3), 191–207.

Tomes, N. (2016). *Remaking the American patient: How Madison Avenue and modern medicine turned patients into consumers.* Chapel Hill: University of North Carolina Press.

Turner, R. J. (2009). Understanding Health Disparities: The Promise of the Stress Process Model. In: Avison W., Aneshensel C., Schieman S., Wheaton B. (eds) *Advances in the Conceptualization of the Stress Process.* Springer, New York, NY.

Van Ryn, M., & Fu, S. (2003). Paved with good intentions: Do public health and human service providers contribute to racial/ethnic disparities in health?. *American Journal of Public Health*, 93(2), 248–255.

Waitzkin, H. (2000). *The second sickness: Contradictions of capitalist health care.* Lanham, MD: Rowman & Littlefield Publishers.

Wallace, M. E., Green, C., Richardson, L., Theall, K., & Crear-Perry, J. (2017). "Look at the whole me": A mixed-methods examination of Black infant mortality in the US through women's lived experiences and community context. *International Journal of Environmental Research and Public Health*, 14(7). https://doi.org/10.3390/ijerph14070727

Washington, H. (2006). *Medical apartheid.* New York: First Anchor Books.

Wechter, M. E., Stewart, E. A., Myers, E. R., Kho, R. M., & Wu, J. M. (2011). Leiomyoma-related hospitalization and surgery: Prevalence and predicted growth based on population trends. *American Journal of Obstetrics and Gynecology, 205*(5), 492.e1–492.e5. https://doi.org/ 10.1016/j.ajog.2011.07.008

Williams, D. R. (1999). Race, socioeconomic status, and health: The added effects of racism and discrimination. *Annals of the New York Academy of Sciences, 896*(1), 173–188.

Williams, D. R. (2012). Miles to go before we sleep: Racial inequities in health. *Journal of Health and Social Behavior, 53*(3), 279–295. https://doi.org/10.1177/0022146512455804

Williams, D. R., & Collins, C. (1995). US socioeconomic and racial differences in health: Patterns and explanations. *Annual Review of Sociology, 21*(1), 349–386.

Williams, D. R., Mohammed, S. A., Leavell, J., & Collins, C. (2010). Race, socioeconomic status, and health: Complexities, ongoing challenges, and research opportunities. *Annals of the New York Academy of Sciences, 1186*(1), 69–101.

Williams, D. R., Priest, N., & Anderson, N. B. (2016). Understanding associations among race, socioeconomic status, and health: Patterns and prospects. *Health Psychology, 35*(4), 407.

Yarbrough, M., & Bennett, C. (1999). Cassandra and the Sistahs: The peculiar treatment of African American women in the myth of women as liars. *Journal of Gender, Race and Justice, 3*, 625–658.

INDEX

abortion, 100–3

African Americans
  distrust of medical establishment by, 66–68,
    69, 117–18
  feeling of need for positive self-presentation, 24
  likelihood of living in racially segregated
    neighborhoods, 20
  preferences for choice of neighborhoods, 86
  social stratification among, 34–35
  sources and use of power within Black
    community, 35
  worse health outcomes compared to similar White
    people, 56
  See also Black middle class; Black middle-class women

ahistoricism, and stereotyping, 117

allostatic load, increased by discrimination, 25–26

American healthcare institutions, as "White
  spaces," 28–29

Anderson, Elijah, 21, 27–28, 37

anti-Black misogyny, 3n3, 39–40, 99–100

"armed with information" coping strategy, 48–54

Aronson, Joshua, 23

Bailey, Moya, 3n3

Bella (study participant)
  effect of structural discrimination on, 54–55
  experiences with reproductive healthcare
    system, 110–11
  impression of healthcare system and providers, 52
  sexual exploitation of, 53–54

Bennett, Dionne, 32

biological differences between races. *See* racial
  essentialism

Black Bourgeoisie (Frazier), 121–22

Black hairdressers, excessive wait times at, 82–83

Black hardiness, 97–98. *See also* racial essentialism

Black healthcare providers
  inability of to mitigate financial and time
    pressures, 73
  inability of to prevent hysterectomy disparities,
    106–8
  as ineffective tool against systematic discrimination,
    5, 113, 114

intraracial tension in patient-provider
    relationships, 80–85
  research on race concordance hypothesis, 57–58
  safety as motivation for preference for, 67
  and stress of racial bias, 28–29
  study participant's experiences with, 59–69

Black Metropolis (Drake and Cayton), 121–22

Black middle class
  definition of, 19–20
  efforts to differentiate themselves from poorer Black
    people, 34–35, 37, 40, 45
  health outcome disparities among, 6–8
  income compared to White counterparts, 94
  intraracial class variation, 14, 37, 80–85
  life chances as similar to Black poor, 18–19
  origin of U.S. stereotypes faced by, 27–29
  stereotypes faced by Black women, 3, 11, 29–34,
    102, 117
  stereotyping and its health effects, 25–26
  stereotyping and the healthcare encounter, 21–24
  struggle of to align inner and outer lives, 17–19
  suggestion of non-existence, 18–19
  theoretical approaches to studying, 34–37
  See also Black middle-class women; race and gender
    concordance

Black middle-class women
  cultural health capital used by, 4, 12, 23, 24, 39,
    45–47, 73–75, 94, 110, 113, 115, 116
  effect of stereotyping on self-concept, 4–5, 32–33, 117
  efforts to connect with doctors, 45–47
  health-related stereotype threat and, 115–17
  income compared to White counterparts, 94
  intersection of race, gender, disability, and age, 77
  intersection of race and gender, 29–31, 88–89
  as misrecognized, 46
  origin of U.S. stereotypes faced by, 27–29
  stereotype of as asexual and self-sacrificing, 32
  stereotype of as emasculating and aggressive, 32–33
  stereotype of as strong, 33–34, 100–1, 116
  stereotypes faced by, 3, 11, 29–34
  struggle of to get best treatment in American
    healthcare system, 113
  See also race and gender concordance; reproductive
    healthcare

Printed in the USA/Agawam, MA
December 28, 2022

803569.003